Pompeii

DUCKWORTH ARCHAEOLOGICAL HISTORIES

Pompeii

Alison E. Cooley

Duckworth

Second impression 2004
First published in 2003 by
Gerald Duckworth & Co. Ltd.
90-93 Cowcross Street, London EC1M 6BF
Tel: 020 7490 7300
Fax: 020 7490 0080
inquiries@duckworth-publishers.co.uk
www.ducknet.co.uk

A catalogue record for this book is available
from the British Library

ISBN 0 7156 3161 6

Typeset by Ray Davies
Printed and bound in Great Britain by
CPI Bath

Contents

For my parents

Acknowledgements

My parents first introduced me to the ruins of Pompeii when I was four. My main memory of this first visit is of being caught in a summer storm, and watching the rainwater sweep down between the stepping-stones in the streets. After several more family visits to the site, it was perhaps inevitable that I ended up studying Pompeii for my D.Phil. thesis under the genial supervision of Greg Woolf and Margareta Steinby. Although this book is not the direct result of that research, many of the debts which I incurred during my doctoral work remain relevant to the writing of it. In particular, the community of the British School at Rome provided an exciting setting for discussing Pompeian studies, not least with Roger Ling, and the process of research was much eased by the librarian Valerie Scott and the secretary Maria Pia Malvezzi. The latter has negotiated many *permessi* for me over the years, and I am also grateful to two successive Soprintendenti of Pompeii, Prof. B. Conticello and Prof. P. Guzzo, for their permission to study parts of the site which are usually closed and to visit the site's archive and storerooms. I also wish to thank Dott.ssa Lista of Naples Museum for providing access to the maze of storerooms there.

In writing this book, I have enjoyed the support and criticism of the series editor Tom Harrison; Deborah Blake of Duckworth has offered advice on many practical problems. Numerous conversations with Joanne Berry about Pompeian problems have been further enriched by her kindness in reading and commenting on the manuscript.

My greatest debt, though, goes to my family. My husband, Melvin, has provided constant encouragement and advice. My parents have been unstinting in their support and have helped me in numerous ways: accompanying me on trips to Pompeii and Naples Museum, taking photographs for use in the book, helping to prepare the maps, and reading countless drafts of the chapters. It seems too small a gesture only to be able to dedicate this book to them.

List of Illustrations

Plates
(between pages 64 and 65)

Figures

Introduction

There has been much calamity in the world, but little that has brought posterity so much pleasure.

J.W. von Goethe, *Italian Journey,* 13 March 1787[1]

This is not a guidebook to the ruins of Pompeii, nor a history of the town in antiquity. Such works already exist in vast numbers, ranging from concise guides to lavish coffee-table books. Instead, it is a history of responses to the ruins, of which Goethe's remark cited above is just one example. As such, it hopes to interest some of the thousands of visitors to the site, who wish to gain some insight into how their own experiences of visiting Pompeii belong to a continuum that dates back to the mid-eighteenth century. Bearing in mind that, compared with 250 years ago, a much greater area of the town has been uncovered for exploration by today's visitors, how else has the experience of touring Pompeii been influenced over the intervening years and what new revelations could the site still hold in store?

Our picture of Pompeii has changed over the years according to the questions people have chosen to ask of the evidence available to them and the issues they have chosen to analyse through new archaeological exploration. The diversity presented by the site, with its paintings and mosaics, its houses and public buildings, its tombs and human remains, has stimulated many different interpretations of the history of the town and its inhabitants since it was first identified as the ill-fated town of Pompeii. There appears to be virtually no limit to the number of questions that could be asked of our archaeological evidence. Past agendas have not been selected in a historical vacuum: often the contemporary political situation has encouraged a particular approach, or advances in science and archaeology have created the opportunity to ask new questions about the site.

This book does not claim to provide a comprehensive history of the excavations, but instead selects a number of particularly significant periods when modern interpretation of the site has been influenced by politics and by advances in archaeological techniques and scientific knowledge. As a result, it omits some of the highlights of Pompeii's excavation history,

11

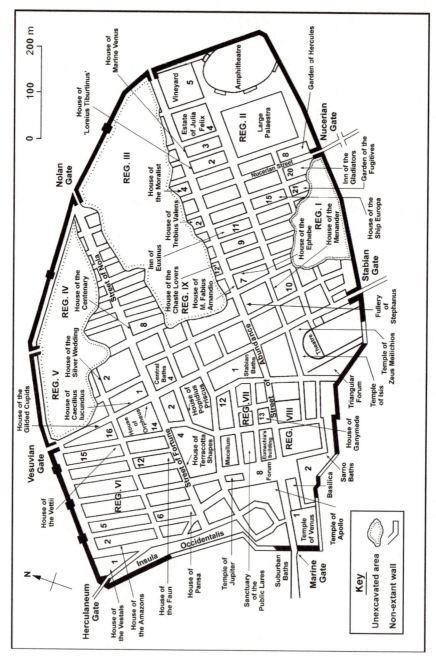

Fig. 1. Map of Pompeii.

such as the discovery by Amedeo Maiuri of the 'Villa of Mysteries' with its controversial paintings, and of the 'House of the Menander' with its impressive silver treasure. Likewise, it deals only briefly with the early twentieth-century project led by Vittorio Spinazzola, which uncovered the lower stretch of 'Street of Abundance', where many insights were gained into the town's commercial and political life. But different people will probably lament the omission of different discoveries. Others, for example, may miss discussion of the unveiling of a whole new area of tombs outside the 'Nucerian Gate' in the 1950s.

The first two chapters trace how advances in seismology and vulcanology have in the last decade or so encouraged archaeologists to re-examine the nature of life at Pompeii in the town's last phase of existence and to set new agendas for their archaeological investigations in relation to the town's eventual destruction in AD 79. As I describe in Chapter 1, in AD 62 the town was at the epicentre of a severe earthquake, which, with the benefit of hindsight, was clearly a preliminary warning of the nightmare which was to unfold when Vesuvius erupted seventeen years later. Long considered to be essentially a period of social and economic decline, recent co-operation between archaeologists and seismologists has resulted in a more complex picture of the period between these natural disasters. In Chapter 2, I reveal how advances in vulcanology have prompted a reconsideration of the progress of the eruption itself. A new awareness of its terrifying violence, mirrored by the eruption of Mount St Helens in 1980, has led to a fresh understanding of its impact upon the formation of the site's archaeological record.

The third chapter explores what might be termed the 'dark ages' of Pompeii, between its destruction in AD 79 and its official rediscovery in 1748. One of the commonest impressions people have of Pompeii is that the town's burial in the eruption sealed it in some sort of time capsule. This impression has been encouraged by discoveries evocative of that last day, like the carbonised loaves of bread found in a baker's oven. Nevertheless, it is now clear that the town did not lie entirely undisturbed over the centuries. The importance of this lies in its implications for what we can expect to uncover – not an untouched mass of evidence, but a site whose sleep has been disturbed over the ages.

In Chapters 4 and 5, I assess the impact of contemporary politics upon the excavations in the eighteenth and nineteenth centuries. The patronage of the earliest excavations by Charles Bourbon, the founder of a new royal dynasty in Naples, resulted in a hunt for artistic treasures in order to boost his international reputation and to confirm his new position of power. From the 1770s, the town became a compulsory stop on the Grand Tour, attracting royalty, writers, and artists alike. Such visitors did not only leave accounts of their impressions of the site, but could even influence the process of excavation in minor ways. The 'discovery' of objects was sometimes staged in order to impress important visitors, who were presented with gifts to remind them of the site. Whereas nowadays visitors keenly purchase replicas as souvenirs, these early visitors actually took away originals! During the nineteenth century, the pace and direction of excavations were directly affected by the political vicissitudes of the time: the Bourbons were exiled and replaced by Napoleon's family, only to return from exile and then be expelled once more as the Risorgimento movement gathered impetus under the leadership of Garibaldi. This heralded a decisive moment for the site, with the emergence of Giuseppe Fiorelli as its new director, who promoted a more systematic and scientific approach not only to excavation, but also crucially to the documentation of the excavations. Furthermore, under Fiorelli's aegis, the site increasingly came to be viewed as a town with a history rather than simply as a treasure-trove of artistic objects.

The last two chapters bring us into the twentieth century. In Chapter 6, I pick out one of the many highlights in twentieth-century archaeology at Pompeii, the revelation of previously hidden gardens in the town. By rediscovering the existence not only of the gardens in rich properties, but also the many market gardens and vineyards within the town's walls, we now have a new picture of the economic and agricultural life of the town. Finally, the last chapter, perhaps paradoxically, goes backwards historically to the period before Pompeii was even a Roman town, before Sulla imposed his colony of veterans upon it in about 80 BC as punishment for the town's resistance to him. This period has only become the object of intensive stratigraphic research in comparatively recent times. Both of these twentieth-century research agendas (investigating the green areas of Pompeii and its pre-Roman history) are the result of modern interest in tracing the urban development of Pompeii, in terms of its historical evolution and as regards land-use in the town. In part too, these new interests represent a response to a major problem faced by the site's directorship today, namely, how to preserve what has already been uncovered. The huge size of the site means that it is a daunting task to cope with maintaining the status quo, simply keeping the weeds at bay, or preventing walls from tumbling down, not least in the aftermath of serious earthquakes, such as that in 1981. Consequently, it might seem a bad idea to continue excavating completely fresh areas of the town on a large scale, when whatever is dug up then has to struggle for survival against the natural elements. By digging down beneath areas already exposed, archaeologists can answer new questions about the town at the same time as leaving significant areas of the site for future generations to excavate, no doubt with the benefit of new scientific and archaeological advances.

Finally, a couple of practical points should be noted before reading the text. I have adopted the usual convention in referring to the location of a house by three numbers (such as I.x.4) whereby the first number (I) represents the region, or *regio*, the second (x) the town-block, or *insula*, and the third (4) the doorway. Individual buildings mentioned appear on the general town map of Pompeii (Fig. 1). I have also tried to identify a house by its most common name, where appropriate, but have not given competing alternatives. In citing bibliographical references in endnotes, where a work also features in the section recommending 'further reading' for that chapter, it appears only by author and short title in the notes. In addition, a glossary of technical terms is provided at the end of the book.

1. Prologue to the Nightmare

We have heard, my dear Lucilius, that Pompeii, a busy town in Campania, situated where the shore of Sorrento and Stabiae from the one side and from the other the shore of Herculaneum come together and encircle with a beautiful bay the sea where it has been brought in from open waters, has subsided under an earthquake. All the surrounding areas have also been affected. What is more, this happened during winter, a time our ancestors used to promise us was free from danger of this kind. This tremor was on the 5th February in the consulship of Regulus and Verginius, and it inflicted great devastation on Campania, a region never safe from this evil, yet which has remained undamaged and has so often got off with a fright. For part of the town of Herculaneum too fell down and even the structures that remain are unstable, and the colony of Nuceria, though it escaped disaster, nevertheless is not without complaint. Naples too lost many private buildings, but no public ones, being stricken only lightly by the great evil; even villas have collapsed, everywhere things shook without injury. In addition, the following events occurred: a flock of six hundred sheep died and statues split, some people have lost their minds and wander about in their madness. Both the texture of my proposed work and the coincidence of the misfortune at this time demand that we explain the reasons for these things.

The Younger Seneca, *Natural Questions* 6.1.1-3

Pompeii owed not only its demise but also its birth and growth to eruptions of Mount Vesuvius. The site chosen for the town's foundation in about the late seventh century BC was a plateau created by a prehistoric lava flow. This gave the town a commanding position on the coast of the Bay of Naples at the mouth of the River Sarno. Its location allowed it to flourish as a river-port, as it acted as an intermediary between the communities along the river valley and the outside world. In addition, its prosperity was also derived from the intensive cultivation of the highly fertile soil which had accumulated over thousands of years thanks to the volcano. The town's growth also owed much to its regional location in Campania (Fig. 2). Ever since Greek cities had set up colonies there, such as Cumae and Pithekoussai, during the mid-eighth century BC, the region of Campania had enjoyed close contacts with the Greek East, developing trading links

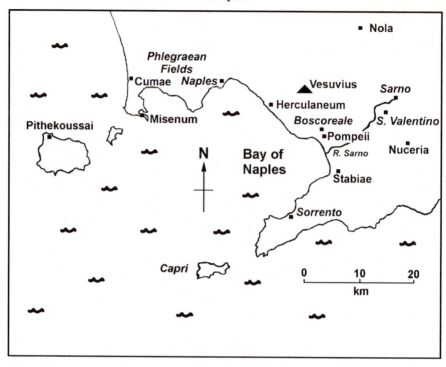

Fig. 2. Map of the Bay of Naples. (Modern names shown in italics.)

and adopting Greek architectural forms. The three temples at Paestum (founded *c.* 600 BC as the Greek colony of Posidonia), for example, remain some of the finest examples anywhere of Greek temple architecture.

Pompeii too, as we shall see later, benefited from extensive cultural and economic links with the Greek East. Indeed, for most of its existence, Pompeii was not a Roman town at all, but was occupied by non-Roman Italic peoples. By the fourth century, Pompeii was part of the Nucerian League, allies who fell into dispute with Rome.[1] The Social War of 91-87 BC, however, led to Pompeii's subjugation to Rome. Italian allies up and down the peninsula, including Pompeii, fought this war against Rome in their quest for full Roman citizenship, and, although they were eventually successful in gaining their demand, various colonies of Roman veteran soldiers were imposed upon Italian towns. One of these, the *Colonia Cornelia Veneria Pompeianorum*, was imposed upon Pompeii in *c.* 80 BC by the great Roman general Sulla as a penalty for the town's earlier resistance against him.[2] As a result, not only did up to two thousand veteran soldiers and their families come to live in Pompeii, but the town's political status changed, its administrative structures were altered, and Latin, rather than the Italic dialect Oscan, became its official language. After this, Pompeii was much more closely affected by activities at Rome: for example, in 62 BC the Pompeians were almost implicated in the 'conspiracy' of Catiline, as revealed by one of Cicero's speeches.[3]

This small but prosperous harbour-town, however, only rarely caught the notice of the élite at Rome, upon whose literary output we rely so often for insights into Roman history. One occasion on which Pompeii, along with its immediate neighbours, did hit the headlines was when the town was rocked by violent earth tremors in AD 62.[4] So destructive were these that they inspired Seneca, the Roman senator and advisor to the emperor Nero, to include an account of earthquakes in his work on natural phenomena entitled *Natural Questions*, which he was composing at that time, and to introduce this account by a description of the Campanian disaster. Seneca's decision to comment on Pompeii owed nothing to the posthumous celebrity of the town, which it achieved at the cost of being buried by Vesuvius, since he himself had been forced to commit suicide by his imperial protégé long before AD 79. His account reveals that Pompeii was near the epicentre of the earthquake and it graphically describes the disruption suffered. Later on in the same work he gives the impression that the earthquake was much talked about: 'Indeed this earthquake, which has filled the world with tales, did not extend beyond Campania' (*Natural Questions* 6.25.3). By contrast, the more laconic notice of the event in Tacitus' *Annals* (15.22) may be largely the result of his knowledge of what happened in 79, which he had already written about in the *Histories* (but not in the part of the text that has survived to the present day): 'Under the same consuls a gymnasium burned down as a result of being struck by lightning, and a statue of Nero in it was melted into shapeless bronze. And the busy town of Pompeii in Campania largely collapsed because of an earthquake; and the Vestal Virgin Laelia died: her place was taken by Cornelia from the family of the Cossi.' Mention of the earthquake here belongs to a section reviewing minor events of the year, typical of Tacitus' annalistic technique, where its literary function is to serve almost as an omen of the troubles yet to come under Nero.[5]

The idea that the town was seriously afflicted by one particular earthquake is also supported by the scenes sculpted on the side of the household shrine, or *lararium*, in the 'House of Caecilius Iucundus' (V.i.26). The relief

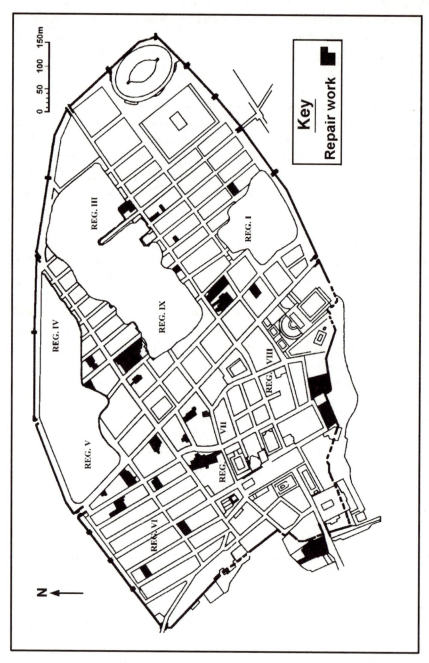

Fig. 3. Pompeii: houses where repair work in AD 79 can be identified.

illustrates a town, whose buildings are recognisably those of Pompeii, being rocked by earth tremors. Unsurprisingly, perhaps, the artist does not offer a strictly accurate representation of the effects of a powerful earthquake, portraying as he does whole buildings sliding over to one side, but he does capture the atmosphere of everything being turned topsy-turvy. The relief is made up of two panels, showing two different areas of the town. These are usually identified as being the centre of civic life, the Forum, and the 'Vesuvian Gate', which is situated just a few hundred yards beyond the house in which the pictures were displayed. One may speculate about the reasons for the *lararium* being decorated in this way: was it perhaps set up as a thank-offering for a member of the family or for the household as a whole having survived the earthquake? Its physical context on the side of a shrine honouring the gods entrusted with protecting the household certainly supports this hypothesis. It seems very likely that the relief does commemorate a particular disaster, and it may indeed be that of AD 62. The problem is, however, that although this primary evidence, together with Seneca's account, offers a valuable contemporary representation of the disaster, it has also over-influenced modern interpretations of earthquake damage at Pompeii. Until recently, any sign of structural damage in the town was thought to be due to 'the earthquake of 62', and the fact that this particular earthquake was identifiable in the historical record, independently of the archaeological record, resulted in the attribution to it of all archaeological signs of damage. The main problem with this assumption is that it has created the impression that the inhabitants of Pompeii were living in a state of crisis from AD 62 to 79. If all evidence for damage and repairs in AD 79 were the result of the earthquake in 62, the fact that repairs had not been completed even seventeen years later would appear to imply that the people of Pompeii lacked either the inclination or the resources to carry them out more quickly.

A variety of structural damage can be seen on the site (Fig. 3). In many places, cracks in walls have been repaired with re-used materials, such as bits of tile and brick. Sometimes unorthodox materials, including fragments of *amphorae* and mosaic, have been used for filling in large wall surfaces. In the 'Insula of the Menander' (I.x), for example, the core of walls constructed in *opus incertum* (where a rubble and mortar core is faced with irregularly shaped medium-sized stones) often contains debris, including bits of bricks and tiles, lumps of waterproof *opus signinum* paving, and pieces of wall-plaster.[6] Many repairs are easily identifiable by an abrupt change in building materials. At one end of town, columns in the Large Palaestra have been strengthened with brick-work and internal corridors within the Amphitheatre reinforced with brick buttressing, while at the other end of the 'Street of Abundance' the last part of the southern façade of the Building of Eumachia along the street, where it abuts the Forum, shows a sudden switch to brick construction (see Plate I).[7]

Elsewhere, we can see that repairs were still in progress in 79. Lime kilns, large piles of gypsum and lime, and the storage of lime in *amphorae*, which have been transformed into cheap, ad hoc containers by breaking off their necks, indicate a range of building work being carried out in different parts of the town. Piles of lime, pieces of mosaic, and sand indicate preparation for re-walling and re-flooring. It also seems likely that the town's water supply was not working at full capacity at the time of the eruption: work in 1992-4 to install modern cabling underneath the site's pavements revealed that in many places trenches linking together the network were full of pumice stones, showing that they had been open to the elements at the time of the eruption.[8] It appears that earthquake damage prompted a complete overhaul of the town's water system, re-installing its lead pipes deeper down than before.

Recent excavation in the 'House of the Chaste Lovers' (IX.xii.6-7), on the northern side of the 'Street of Abundance', has even revealed preliminary work in progress on wall decoration, and the ancient equivalent of paint pots standing on the floor – *amphora* bases containing the remnants of pigment. Admittedly, we cannot simply assume that a decision to redecorate the house was necessarily a direct response to earthquake damage. Nevertheless, both this house and the adjacent bakery appear to have been undergoing a major programme of restructuring in 79: millstones were found in a dismantled state, and several heaps of lime were scattered around. Significantly, though, the bakery was still in use, as indicated by the discovery of the remains of seven mules, whose job it would have been to turn the mills, tethered in the stable. Their carbonised feed was found elsewhere, while the kitchen hearth also retained the debris from a recent meal of a piglet and bird. Clearly it was business as usual despite the building work.[9]

Nor was it only private buildings that were discovered in an incompletely renovated state. Only part of the podium of the 'Temple of Venus' had been built, and stone was found stockpiled and cut in readiness for use in the temple's podium and walls, along with some marble entablature pieces and a half-finished Corinthian capital. Similarly, the vaulted roofs in the warm-room (*tepidarium*) and hot-room (*caldarium*) of the men's section of the Stabian Baths remained in a state of disrepair.[10]

Of course, any town, whether ancient or modern, is always full of building-work, which need not be prompted by earth tremors. How different would Pompeii look to us today if Vesuvius had erupted a hundred years earlier? We would still come across piles of building materials, half-finished structures, and redecoration in progress.

Only in the last couple of decades have archaeologists begun to question the common assumption that all structural damage at Pompeii must be a direct consequence of the major earthquake in 62. A new approach to the archaeological evidence has been encouraged by the work of seismologists and vulcanologists, which has suggested that it is highly unlikely that Pompeii suffered only from a single major earthquake. Instead, scientists argue that the town was probably damaged by a series of earth tremors in the period leading up to the eruption.[11] Prompted by this, closer examination by archaeologists has revealed that even structures apparently built afresh after the earthquake were, in turn, damaged at some point before 79 (Fig. 4). For example, it is generally agreed that the Central Baths were begun only after 62, on land made available by the demolition of houses damaged in the earthquake.[12] These baths were still being constructed in 79, with a number of elements indicating work in progress, notably the way in which rooms had been built up only to the springing of their vaults, and the discovery of four Doric capitals in various stages of completion. Nevertheless, the east wall of the hot-room (*caldarium*) shows signs of already having been repaired and reinforced by 79.[13] Furthermore, in both the 'House of the Gilded Cupids' (VI.xvi.7) and the 'House of Fabius Rufus' (VII *insula occidentalis* 19-23), it appears that initial damage was repaired, damaged again, and again repaired.[14] Recent study of the 'Insula of the Menander' (I.x), carried out with these questions in mind, has also identified possible places where structural damage might be due to earth tremors after 62.[15] For example, recently completed decoration in the peristyle area of the 'House of the Menander' (I.x.4) shows signs of damage. It is impossible, however, to be sure that cracks in walls were caused by later earth tremors rather than by the long-term effects of the major earthquake, with cracks forming as the buildings' foundations gradually settled down again. Now that archaeologists are no longer automatically attributing all signs of damage to one big earthquake, it is likely that further cases of post-62 damage and repair will be identified.

In this way, our picture of Pompeii in its last few years of existence from

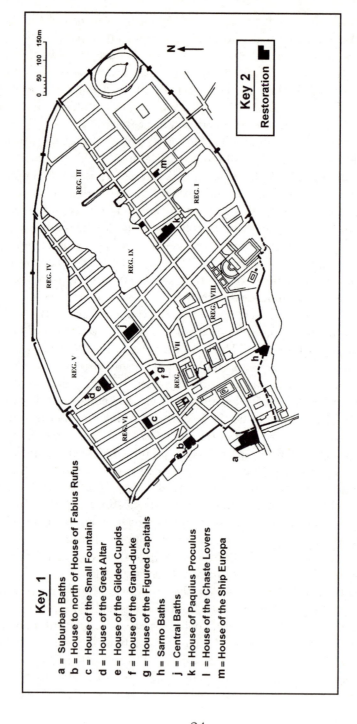

Key 1

a = Suburban Baths
b = House to north of House of Fabius Rufus
c = House of the Small Fountain
d = House of the Great Altar
e = House of the Gilded Cupids
f = House of the Grand-duke
g = House of the Figured Capitals
h = Sarno Baths
j = Central Baths
k = House of Paquius Proculus
l = House of the Chaste Lovers
m = House of the Ship Europa

Key 2
Restoration

REG. III
REG. IV
REG. V
REG. VI
REG. VII
REG. VIII
REG. IX
REG. I

N

0   50   100   150m

Fig. 4. Pompeii: locations of restorations to walls already rebuilt after AD 62.

62 to 79 has been radically altered through new archaeological investigation into questions that have been reconfigured in response to modern scientific knowledge about the relationship of earthquakes and volcanic eruptions. The archaeological evidence is, in fact, much more complicated than scholars previously thought. A range of possibilities now opens up for explaining damage: it might be due to the earthquake of 62, to subsequent tremors between 62 and 79, or to the violence of the eruption itself. This now makes more sense scientifically, since a major eruption is commonly preceded by earth tremors over some time, heralding the disturbance of tectonic plates deep within the earth, which eventually cause the eruption itself. Earthquakes during the previous six months heralded Vesuvius' explosive eruption on 16 December 1631. Furthermore, we know from one of the famous letters written by Pliny the Younger, who witnessed the eruption from across the Bay of Naples, that the eruption of 79 was also preceded by a series of damaging shocks: 'There had been tremors for many days previously, a common occurrence in Campania and no cause for panic, but that night they strengthened so that everything seemed not so much shaken as overturned' (*Letters* 6.20.3).

We may be sure that the town was affected by seismic shocks during this final period in its history. Quite how life was affected, however, is a matter for dispute. If we start with the archaeological evidence, it is no longer self-evident that the non-completion of repair work is a sign of crisis, with the town's inhabitants being financially incapable of undertaking adequate repair works, or lacking the interest to do so. On the contrary, it could be suspected that the large volume of evidence for repairs indicates quite the opposite, that the inhabitants of Pompeii were investing heavily in repairing their town. Nor was it necessarily the case that the pace of repair was so slow that damage caused in 62 still had not been repaired in 79. Admittedly, many Pompeians were living in far from pristine conditions in the period leading up to 79, but many of them were actively engaged in repairing and improving their homes. Besides, we should not assume that buildings that remained incompletely repaired were not in use. One house where repairs were being carried out, for example, was still being used as a gem-cutter's workshop (II.ix.2): two wooden boxes contained the cutter's on-going work, with one holding gems ready for sale, and the other, gems still incompletely cut.[16] The possibility that incompletely repaired buildings might still be being used will be an important consideration in assessing the state of the Forum in 79 a little later in this chapter.

One particular episode in the excavation of the site offers us a vivid impression of the town's continued vitality during the period leading up to the eruption. This was the excavation of the lower, eastern section of the 'Street of Abundance' carried out by Vittorio Spinazzola, the site's director from 1911 to 1923. This street was one of the main roads through the town, leading from the Forum to the Amphitheatre, so we would expect to find it teeming with activity. In addition, however, the lively picture it conjures up of trade, commerce, politics, and recreation is the result of the way in which it was excavated. The decision to restore balconies on I.xi/xii recaptures a better impression of what the town may have looked like. Painted electoral campaigning notices and advertisements for forthcoming shows in the Amphitheatre have been left in situ. Alongside these are other paintings relating to the workshops opening onto the street, reflecting the owners' aspirations for their businesses to prosper. One of these, on the façade of a felt-workshop (IX.vii.5-7), depicts Mercury, patron-god of commerce, emerging from a temple clutching a moneybag.[17] It is also the preservation and recording of different types of evidence that helps to recreate the busy atmosphere. In the case of the 'fullery of Stephanus' (I.vi.7), uncovered in 1912-14, Spinazzola's team uncovered not only the basins, press, and drying-terrace used in the fulling process, but also the pots and gridiron in the kitchen. In addition to revealing insights into the fullers at work, cleaning and finishing items of clothing, the excavations further provided a sense of the fullers' broader contribution to town-life: outside, on the workshop's façade, an electoral painted notice advertised their unanimous support of a candidate for local office.[18]

Paradoxically, perhaps, it was partly this type of evidence for a lively commercial scene on the 'Street of Abundance' that led to a long tradition of interpreting Pompeian society after 62 as being rather degenerate in character, as it became increasingly plebeian and interested in commerce. It is suggested that many of the élite left the town altogether, leaving it in the hands of the lower classes, with the result that manumitted slaves, or freedmen, assumed a more prominent role in society than they had previously enjoyed. In part, this idea of migration is derived from Seneca, who suggests 'Let us cease listening to those who have turned their backs on Campania, and who have emigrated after this misfortune, and say that they will never go to that region in future' (*Natural Questions* 6.1.10). Much of this picture, however, depends upon what now appears to be an outdated interpretation of the significance of 'the earthquake of 62'. It also ignores the way in which the rise of freedmen is typical of Roman society as a whole during this period, with imperial freedmen in the courts of Claudius and Nero leading the way at Rome.

The picture of Pompeian society from 62 to 79 which has been dominant until recently is that formulated during the 1940s by Amedeo Maiuri, the site's director from 1924 to 1960, whose excavations transformed our image of the town, not least by uncovering the 'House of the Menander' (I.x.4) and the 'Villa of Mysteries'. He argued that the damage caused by the earthquake to what he termed 'patrician' houses plunged the élite into a state of financial crisis. Being forced to sell or rent out their rich residences, which were promptly converted into workshops or smaller units of habitation, the élite was compelled to yield before the inexorable rise of a newly powerful commercial class. In his view, at least some of the élite, including the owner of the 'House of the Menander' (I.x.4), moved out of Pompeii as a result, leaving it in the hands of the lower commercial classes, notably freedmen.[19]

Recent archaeological discoveries, however, allow us to challenge this view of the élite's abandonment of the town. The tomb enclosure of one of Pompeii's most prominent families during the Neronian period, the Lucretii Valentes, has recently been uncovered a little way beyond the town towards the south-east, in the modern district of Scafati.[20] The inscriptions found in the tomb complement graffiti and painted inscriptions in Pompeii in demonstrating how this family continued to play a leading role in public life even after the earthquake. Their town-house, the 'House of Marine Venus' (II.iii.3), is identifiable on the basis of graffiti wishing luck to the family scratched inside the house, such as 'Good luck to Decimus, Iusta, and their children', inscribed on the shrine in the peristyle, and also 'Good luck to Satrius, good luck to Iusta, good luck to Valentina, good luck to Decimus Lucretius Valens junior'.[21] In several painted inscriptions, the Lucretii Valentes were celebrated for the lavish gladiatorial shows they gave in the Amphitheatre, and it seems that Lucretius Valens junior, whose dead infant son represents the youngest generation of the family known to us, probably stood for election to the post of aedile between 62 and 68/69.[22] The family's involvement in public life, therefore, seems not to have abated at all in this final period of the town's existence, when they were also apparently still living in the town. Admittedly, this is only one family, but their example warns us not to accept without hesitation a picture of the widespread migration of Pompeii's élite after 62.

The crisis theory has been used to explain a striking feature of urban change during the last phase of life at Pompeii, namely the conversion of houses into fulleries and other workshops. For example, bakeries take over houses at VII.ii.3, V.iii.8, and VI.iii.3; in VII.ii.11 basins for dyeing are inserted into a portico; and a house at I.vi.7 is converted into a fullery.[23] This archaeological evidence is taken as indicating the presence of a larger number of the lower classes (craftsmen and workmen) in the town than formerly, and this is attributed directly to the effects of 'the earthquake'.[24] A further example, the transformation of a house into a shop selling fish sauce (*garum*) (I.xii.8), reveals the potential feebleness of this picture, however, since its transformation cannot be dated with any certainty, but could have happened at any point during the first century AD.[25] This raises the possibility that such adaptations of domestic space for commercial usage may not have been related to 'the earthquake' at all. After all, we do not know exactly when many of these houses were converted, since they have generally been analysed only on the basis of their standing structures, without testing when they were converted by stratigraphic excavation.

Furthermore, study of artefacts found in a sample of houses suggests that it was not uncommon for Pompeian houses to serve both as a home and as a place of business or production.[26] Modern reactions to the mixture of domestic and commercial architecture may be anachronistic, therefore, in assuming that Pompeians too would have viewed the two spheres of activity as mutually exclusive. Maiuri's distaste for the conversion of 'patrician' houses into workshops also derived from his assumption that the rich were being forced to sell or rent out their town houses because of their financial crisis following the earthquake. It is much more likely, however, that such exploitation of urban property was a deliberate strategy adopted by the élite, who created for themselves a mixed portfolio of economic interests, avoiding in this way any risks inherent in relying on revenue derived exclusively from agriculture and land-owning.[27]

The emerging dominance of the freedman class has been detected in the rise to social respectability of one family in particular. A six-year-old boy, Numerius Popidius Celsinus, paid for the rebuilding of the Temple of Isis following earthquake damage, and was rewarded by being co-opted into the local council.[28] His father, Numerius Popidius Ampliatus, appears to have been a freedman, for whom membership of the council was prohibited by law. From this one example, a freedman's son is seen to have taken on the role of a public benefactor, which, as far as we can tell, had previously been the preserve of the élite. This case of the social promotion of a particular family (who incidentally had been freed by one of the leading families in the town) is not necessarily indicative of a response to some sort of crisis in society following the earthquake, but is in fact typical of a much wider social pattern, where families drifted in and out of the élite. The élite of Pompeii was not a fixed group of families; rather, each family belonging to the élite had to make a conscious effort to retain its position in society, and it was always possible for new families to climb up the social ladder.[29] Maiuri's picture implies a somewhat static view of the town's social structure, whereby it is assumed that once a family attained a position among the local élite, it always retained that position; the real situation was much more dynamic, with the composition of the élite changing over time.[30]

It is possible to take the picture of a social crisis at Pompeii to extremes, with the suggestion that squatters moved in to many parts of the town after the property-owners themselves had left.[31] This suggestion has arisen from apparent anomalies in the placement of artefacts, as revealed by the archaeological record, and also, quite rightly, from a desire to quash the idea that Pompeii presents some sort of archaeological dream-world, a time capsule where the reality of one day in August 79 is mirrored exactly. As we shall see, however, some of the disruption caused to the deposition of objects must have been due to the eruption itself, and other objects may only appear to be out of place to modern eyes but may have seemed perfectly in place originally. The presence in the peristyle of the 'House of Trebius Valens' (III.ii.1) of a travertine statue base whose inscription reveals that it had once supported a magistrate's statue does not imply that the owners of the house salvaged it illegally from the Forum during the state of civic disorder. On the contrary, the recycling of inscribed monuments in Pompeii is far from unusual; no exceptional circumstances need be invoked to explain it. To give just one example, even the large dedicatory inscription set up above the rear entrance to Eumachia's Building on the Forum in the early first century AD is not a fresh piece of marble, but re-cuts and re-uses an earlier public inscription, which is still preserved on its reverse.[32] Similarly, the idea that a statuette of Apollo found in the peristyle of the 'House of the Menander' (I.x.4) had originally been set up in the Temple of Apollo and had been appropriated after the earthquake is rather anachronistic. There is no evidence that this statuette had ever been displayed in the temple, whereas it could easily have been set up as an ornament in the house.

Nevertheless, the oddity of the location of some groups of artefacts should not be underplayed: the evidence indicates that spaces in houses were not always used as we might expect. A striking photographic image from excavations in the 1950s shows a pile of *amphorae* heaped up in an *impluvium*, which we would more readily think of as an ornamental pool.[33] At least some of the apparent oddity of the archaeological evidence can be explained by the complex patterns of room usage, whereby rooms hosted many different types of activities, rather than by a fundamental change in the composition of society during this final period of the town's existence, prompted by the disruption caused by 'the earthquake' of 62.[34] However, equally important is the acknowledgement that our perception of Pompeian domestic space may be quite different from the ways in which its original inhabitants experienced it.[35] Our tendency to trace room-types, and, by extension, room functions on the basis of names drawn from literary sources, such as Vitruvius' *On Architecture*, provides us with little insight into actual contemporary Pompeian practice. Besides, perceptions of domestic space and concepts of privacy during the first century AD are likely to bear little resemblance to the connotations summoned up by labels commonly in use in modern guidebooks to Pompeian houses, such as 'dining-room', or 'bedroom'. Artefacts at Pompeii, therefore, present us with a complex picture, but do not support the idea that the town was abandoned by the élite in its final years.

Another piece of evidence generally used to support the view that Pompeii was in a state of emergency following the earthquake is the intervention of an agent, Titus Suedius Clemens, appointed by the emperor Vespasian himself to sort out the allocation of land in the town. Four identical limestone inscribed markers have been discovered just outside four of the town's gates – the 'Marine Gate', 'Herculaneum Gate', 'Vesuvian Gate', and 'Nucerian Gate' – and it seems likely that others remain to be found beyond the rest of the gates too: 'By authority of the Emperor Vespasian, Titus Suedius Clemens, Tribune, having carried out a judicial inquiry into the cases and having completed surveys, restored to the Pompeian state public lands appropriated by private individuals' (Plate II).[36] These inscriptions reveal that there had been a problem at Pompeii of individuals usurping public lands, and that Suedius Clemens was appointed to an extraordinary post by the emperor to judge claims to land. Maiuri regarded these measures taken by Suedius Clemens as rather singular, and thought that they represented a response to the usurpation of public land by private individuals taking advantage of the confusion and destruction of public records caused by the earthquake.[37] It is tempting to link the confusion over land boundaries with chaos caused by earth

tremors, but in fact if we set the Pompeian evidence into its wider historical context, an alternative interpretation suggests itself. Instead of
viewing the situation in Pompeii as peculiar to that town alone and the
result of specific local circumstances, we can set it into the wider historical
context of Vespasian's concern with improving public finances in the wake
of the civil wars in AD 68-69, by recovering public lands illegally appropriated by private individuals. A series of inscriptions set up in various parts
of the empire testify to actions by Vespasian himself or by his agents in
re-establishing the boundaries of public lands. The reallocation of lands at
Pompeii can be compared with the activity behind the drawing up of the
land-surveying maps at Orange in modern Provence in AD 77. Other
inscriptions record how Vespasian commissioned the investigation of former boundaries and reclaimed public lands in North Africa, France, and
elsewhere in Italy too. The activity of Suedius Clemens, then, does not
indicate a unique crisis at Pompeii, but an initiative from the emperor to
improve public finances throughout the empire.[38]

As part of the general picture of the disruption caused by the earthquake, scholars have suggested that the inhabitants of Pompeii came to
adopt rather singular priorities in restoring their town. The fact that the
Temple of Isis was already fully restored, but that other temples such as
the 'Temple of Venus' were still unfinished in 79, is taken to indicate that
'traditional cults' were in decline.[39] Such an interpretation fails to explain
satisfactorily why the cult of Isis, established here in the second century
BC, should not also be considered one of Pompeii's 'traditional cults'. Some
have further argued, with respect to the town as a whole, that there were
three different levels of repair amongst the public buildings. First, out of
the public buildings in the town, only the Amphitheatre and the Temple of
Isis were fully restored; secondly the municipal buildings on the south side
of the Forum, together with the Forum Baths, were being used, even
though they had not been completely restored; and lastly, all the other
public buildings (including most of the Forum) were not being used, nor
were they fully restored.[40] In particular, it has been suggested that the
Pompeians neglected the Forum, abandoning it in favour of a temporary
piazza outside the Stabian Baths.[41]

Those who claim that the Forum had been abandoned in confusion
argue that the condition of the area as found on excavation indicated that
the Forum was still in a state of disrepair in AD 79. In particular, the lack
of slabs of marble for revetment, along with the dearth of statues and
inscriptions, might seem to indicate that the Forum had not been fully

restored. The influential nineteenth-century scholar August Mau was convinced that the Forum had been incompletely repaired. He suggested that the scattering of architectural fragments over the Forum's piazza was the result of their being stored there ready for re-use in reconstructing the portico.[42] He also argued that the Temple of Jupiter was being used as a marble-workers' shop after the earthquake, pointing out that a colossal, highly polished marble torso, apparently belonging to the seated cult statue of Jupiter found in the temple, has a rough relief of two figures on its reverse side (Plates III and IV).[43] He supposed this to be the result of a reworking of the torso after the statue was damaged in AD 62, but it is actually much more likely that the relief on the back pre-dates the statue.[44] Three main reasons may be given for this. First, although at first glance the relief does look unfinished, it may in fact have been completed and then chiselled back when re-used for the torso. A small column carved at the lower right side of the relief provides support for this view: it was apparently completed by the addition of flutes, but only the two flutes nearest to the surface of the relief survived the process of chiselling-back, which destroyed the other three. Secondly, the overall shape of the relief does not fit comfortably onto the piece of marble, whereas the torso makes full use of the available space, suggesting that the marble has been re-cut to accommodate it. Lastly, the three dowel-holes for affixing the torso to something else, perhaps a throne or a wall, can be seen in the surface of the relief on the back.

Mau also based his suggestion on what seemed to him a rather strange assemblage of inscriptions and sculpture in the temple. A semi-colossal foot, a colossal mask, the marble head of a woman, and various fragments of statues, such as hands and pieces of toga, were found among the ruins of the *cella*. The inscribed monuments included a dedication to Jupiter on behalf of the welfare of the emperor Gaius Caligula, and a statue base from the Claudian era.[45] The statue base is not honorific in nature, but dedicatory: its inscribed text reveals that Spurius Turranius set up a statue in the *cella*, by permission of the decurions. The inscribed monuments may be explained as votive dedications, therefore, and the same may be true of the pieces of sculpture, of which only fragments have been recovered and recorded.

The final element in the traditional picture, which sees the Temple of Jupiter as a sculptors' workshop and not as a temple in this last period, is the suggestion that its cult was transferred to the smaller 'Temple of Zeus Meilichios'. Three terracotta statuettes found in this small temple, which can be identified as Jupiter, Juno, and Minerva (although other identifications are also possible), seemed to intimate that after the original large cult statues had been damaged, these small figures were used as a stop-gap measure, so that the cult was not neglected altogether, but was simply transferred to a new location.[46] The recent discovery of another small temple beyond the walls of Pompeii in the Fondo Iozzino, which has in turn been identified as the Temple of Zeus Meilichios which we know from an Oscan inscription existed somewhere in this general area, undermines the plausibility of the idea that the worship of Jupiter was transferred from his main civic temple to a more minor one associated with him in a different guise. What has up to now been known as the 'Temple of Zeus Meilichios' seems more likely to have been a temple to Aesculapius.[47]

By contrast, a recent analysis of the Forum concludes that it had been repaired and was in full working order in AD 79.[48] Confusion about the Forum's excavated state is due to the activities of ancient salvagers who returned after the eruption to rescue as much precious material from the site as possible, and, besides, tremors accompanying the eruption must have caused some of the structural damage. The Forum may have been an easy target for salvaging activities, if some of its tall buildings protruded through the destruction layer. The unroofed character of the Forum's piazza must also have facilitated access to the original level.

How are we to reconcile this new picture of a perfect Forum with Mau's image of chaos? Sometimes small, but far from insignificant, pieces of evidence have been ignored in discussing this problem. The claim that only the pedestals of honorific statues decorating the Forum survived can be countered by excavation reports, which mention the discovery of several pieces of statuary from different parts of the Forum.[49] First, the discovery of substantial fragments (a foot with part of a leg, two front legs of a horse, a piece of drapery perhaps from a cloak) of a gilded bronze equestrian statue just outside the Basilica might support the idea that the Forum had been repaired, since such a statue is unlikely to have been left lying around; it would have been melted down or moved to an enclosed area.[50] Two bronze fingers from statues were found on the north side of the Forum beside the Temple of Jupiter, and parts of a marble statue (a left shoulder and arm, a right knee and part of a leg, and a shoulder with cloak) were recovered outside the Basilica.[51] Finally, in excavating the east side of the Forum, in other words along the portico where so many bases remain today, some fragments of statues were found, including a right foot still attached to part of its base and a spear point of gilded bronze.[52] The reporter of the time expressed the hope that they would subsequently discover some whole statues intact, but this hope was apparently never realised. As we shall see in more detail in Chapter 3, extensive salvaging of precious materials from the site occurred during the period from 79 to 1748, the year when 'official' excavations began. All that remains today are the bases, which preserve on their upper surfaces the marks of the clamps which once kept the statues in place.

The claim that there was a lack of material found in the Forum is also questionable. The excavation reports relate that so many pieces of plain and decorative marble were found that a special storeroom was set up to prevent the roads around the Forum from becoming too encumbered with the material. This reveals that large quantities of marble revetment as well as fragments of inscriptions, architecture, and sculpture were discovered. It was even suggested at the time of excavation that perhaps it would be a good idea to try to put some of the fragments together to form whole inscriptions![53] One hundred and eight fragments of marble were subsequently transferred to Naples from the various stores on site, with the result that some remained unrecorded.[54] A brief comment in the reports gives some idea of the problems encountered at the time of excavation. The writer records that a large amount of marble was found in one of the buildings at the south end of the Forum, and that subsequently he recommended that the building be made secure as a modern store for the marble, for fear that it might be stolen.[55] This comment hints at some of the difficulties encountered by the early excavators in protecting their excavated material and implies that the salvaging of precious material might be a relatively modern as well as an ancient phenomenon, contributing further to the denuding of the Forum.

Although it is likely that the Forum had been extensively repaired by the time of the eruption, it would be simplistic to argue that it was in a perfect state. Some repair work was still in progress. In the large public building facing onto the Forum, called the Building of Eumachia, building materials were found, where they had been stockpiled ready for use. A pile of sixteen marble slabs of uniform size was found in a side room in this building.[56] This may be an indication that some sort of revetment work was being prepared. It is, however, wrong to argue that the Forum had to be in perfect condition in order for it to have been operating. Just as private houses were being used even though they had not been completely repaired, the same may be true of the Forum. Is it the fault of 'the earthquake' that we readily accept the notion of incompleteness? The Forum was continually undergoing changes. Just as private property at Pompeii underwent rapid changes, so public space was also constantly changing, particularly the Forum, where different individuals could make their mark by setting up monuments and by being honoured with statues. The Forum was largely, but not necessarily completely, repaired by AD 79, but it did not remain out of action for over a decade. Rather than viewing its incompleteness in 79 as a sign of civic crisis, it may actually have been in the process of being slowly transformed into an even grander centre for public life than before, and indicate exactly the opposite, that the Pompeians still regarded the monumental centre of civic life as crucial to their sense of pride as a community. All this, however, was doomed to come to an abrupt end.

2. The Nightmare Revealed

Mount Vesuvius is situated above these places and people live all around on very beautiful farms, except at the summit. This is largely level, but completely unfruitful, like ashes to look at, and it displays porous hollows of sooty rocks on the surface, as if devoured by fire. As a result, one would deduce that this area was previously on fire and held craters of fire, and that it was extinguished when the fuel failed.

Strabo, *Geography* 5.4.8

It has sometimes been suggested that the Romans were unaware that Vesuvius was a volcano. As the passage cited above demonstrates, however, only a few generations before the eruption in AD 79, the geographical writer Strabo recorded that there was something curious about the summit of the mountain. Similarly, the Sicilian Diodorus, also writing towards the end of the first century BC, compared Vesuvius with Mount Etna back home (4.21.5). Of course, this knowledge may have circulated only among specialists, but even if the local inhabitants had been aware of the mountain's dangerous properties, it is unlikely that anyone would have done anything about it. After all, people today are only too aware of the potential dangers, and yet the region remains densely populated by about three million inhabitants, of whom one million live within a seven-kilometre (just over four-mile) radius of the volcano. This is the area that could be completely destroyed within the first fifteen minutes of a medium-to-large-scale eruption.[1]

Since AD 79, Vesuvius has erupted over thirty times, most violently on 16 December 1631, when the region was shaken by earth tremors for six months beforehand, and most recently in 1944 in the wake of the allied landings.[2] It was, however, the explosive eruption of Mount Pelée on Martinique (West Indies) on 8 May 1902 which first prompted speculation on the full horror of Vesuvius' most notorious eruption. Only three of the 28,000 inhabitants of St Pierre, known as the 'Paris of the West Indies', survived: a little girl who had been sent on an errand, a man whose house was on the edge of the line of destruction, and a prisoner protected by the thick walls of his cell, who subsequently made his living as a side-show attraction at the Barnum and Bailey Circus. Otherwise, the Neapolitan captain of an Italian ship, Marino Leboffe, rescued his crew by ignoring the prohibition on sailing imposed by the port authorities, observing, 'I know nothing about Mount Pelée, but if Vesuvius were looking the way your volcano looks this morning, I'd get out of Naples.' All the other inhabitants were instantly killed by a ground surge (a cloud of hot gas and debris at 700°C) that overwhelmed them at speeds of over 100 km per hour.[3] Although, therefore, the possibility had already been raised that Vesuvius' eruption in 79 had been on a quite different scale of violence from those in modern times, its true horror came to be appreciated fully only in the light of the eruption of Mount St Helens in the north-western United States on 18 May 1980, and also as a result of new archaeological research.

The new interest among archaeologists in reconstructing the course of the eruption in detail has developed hand-in-hand with advances in vulcanology. As well as being of interest for its own sake, this topic is relevant for our understanding of how the archaeological record was itself created. Much is at stake, since the nature of the eruption governed both what was left behind for archaeologists to dig up, and how it was sealed by the deposits from the volcano. On a basic level, for example, it is not valid to derive a pattern for the everyday use of coinage in the town from coins found next to skeletons. Such collections of coins often include more gold and silver coins than bronze denominations. This is a reflection of the victims' attempts to salvage as much worldly wealth as possible, rather than to equip themselves for a day's shopping. By contrast, bronze coins are more prominent in other types of contexts not connected with bodies, such as in houses and shops.[4] The significance of our new understanding of the eruption is much more far-reaching than this, since, instead of supposing that the destruction of Pompeii was caused primarily by the fall of pumice and ash, we can now trace the impact of far more violent forces. The crux of the matter is an appreciation that Vesuvius' eruption in 79 was highly explosive, accompanied by pyroclastic activity. In the last couple of decades, archaeologists and vulcanologists have collaborated in seeking to understand the main outline of events during the eruption, and recent painstaking excavations have permitted a more detailed picture of these events to be recreated. Research into the precise sequence of events continues, but given the important implications of the work so far resulting from dialogue between archaeologists and vulcanologists, it seems opportune to provide a brief account of what seems to be the consensus at the moment.

Time chart of the eruption

24 August

late morning	Eruption begins with phreatomagmatic explosion: thin layer of ash.
	Formation of eruptive column resembling umbrella pine.
early afternoon	'Plinian' phase. Phonolitic magma (white pumice) begins to fall, borne to the south of Vesuvius by prevailing winds.
5-6 pm	At Pompeii, buildings begin to collapse under weight of accumulated pumice; some people try to flee, others take refuge inside houses
8 pm	Magma composition changes to tephritic phonolite (grey pumice).

25 August

early hours	Eruptive column reaches highest point ($c.$ 32 km), maximum discharge of magma: 1.5×10^8 kg/s.
1-2.15 am	Pyroclastic phase. Column collapses. Surges 1-2 overwhelm Herculaneum, reach Oplontis and Boscoreale.
2.15-6.30 am	Grey pumice fall; lull at Pompeii: people try to leave shelter, head towards the south. Column rises again to $c.$ 30 km.
6.30-8 am	Column collapses. Surges 3-6 swoop down over Pompeii within a couple of hours. Surge 3 extends to north wall; Surges 4-6 cover the whole town, bringing death to all remaining in the area. Surge 6 reaches as far as Stabiae.
from 8 am	Final phase of pumice fall; caldera collapse and phreatomagmatic activity.

The most important revelation has been that the eruption consisted of two major phases, with a brief lull in activity in between them. The first phase started on the morning of 24 August, and is named 'Plinian' after the famous eye-witness accounts written by the Younger Pliny in letters to Tacitus (6.16, 6.20).[5] This lasted for about twenty hours, gradually creating a layer of pumice 2.8 metres (over nine feet) thick over Pompeii. After a lull in activity during the early hours of the following morning, a second phase began which was much more violent and destructive. Whereas previously it was thought that the town's inhabitants were killed by the rapid fall of ash and pumice, it is now believed that the first stage of the eruption resulted in relatively few casualties. Indeed, many people may even have escaped to safety during this phase. New analysis of the eruption suggests instead that most of the victims of Vesuvius were overwhelmed during the second stage by the pyroclastic surges and flows that swept down from the volcano.

2. The Nightmare Revealed

The two letters of Pliny provide a first-hand account (albeit one written some years later) of the eruption as experienced by survivors at Stabiae to the south, and as seen by Pliny himself thirty kilometres (over eighteen miles) to the west.[6] The Younger Pliny, then a teenager, had been staying with his uncle (the Elder Pliny) at Misenum, a promontory on the northern side of the Bay of Naples. His uncle had a particular interest in natural phenomena, having just finished writing an encyclopaedic *Natural History* in thirty-seven volumes. The Elder Pliny lost his life in the eruption, as he attempted to rescue a family friend who lived at the foot of the volcano.

Many years later, the historian Tacitus sent the Younger Pliny a request for information about his uncle's death, which he wanted to include in the history that he was then writing. Pliny's letters are particularly valuable in that they provide two different geographical perspectives on the eruption, and describe a survivor's view of the calamity. His first letter reveals that the umbrella-pine-shaped cloud above the volcano was first noticed at about 1 pm:

> My uncle was at Misenum in his capacity as commander of the fleet. On 24 August, at about the seventh hour [i.e. *c*. 1 pm], my mother pointed out to him that a cloud of unusual size and form was appearing. ... He called for his sandals and climbed to the place from which he would have had the best view of the phenomenon. A cloud was rising up – as we were observing from some distance it was unclear from which mountain (afterwards we learnt that it was Vesuvius) – whose likeness and shape a pine tree, of all trees, might best sum up. For, having been lifted up to a great height on a very long 'trunk', it was spreading out in various 'branches'. This was, I believe, because it was lifted up by the fresh blast, then as that died down, defeated by its own weight, it began to disperse far and wide. Sometimes it was white, sometimes dirty and speckled, according to how much mud or ash it had raised up. To a man of my uncle's great intellect, it seemed important and worth learning about from closer at hand.
>
> *Letters* 6.16.4-7

The presence of a thin deposit of ash up to fifteen centimetres (about six inches) deep over an extensive area of up to twenty kilometres (over twelve miles) downwind from the volcano suggests that the explosion which produced this cloud may not have marked the very start of the eruption.[7] This may help to explain how a slave sent by Rectina, a friend of the Elder Pliny who lived near the volcano, to ask his help in escaping, reached Misenum by early afternoon, if she had immediately responded in alarm to a relatively minor start to the eruption.

It has been calculated that the volcano exploded with immense force, such that magma and ash were vomited forth to heights of twenty to thirty kilometres (more than 65,000 to 95,000 feet) above the volcano's vent, under the force of highly pressurised gases.[8] Some sense of the extraordinary character of such a blast may be gained by comparison with the initial explosion of Mount St Helens, which has been calculated as the equivalent of a ten-megaton bomb, or five hundred times the size of the one that devastated Hiroshima.[9] The stratospheric height of the eruptive column over two thousand years ago has been established by examining the relative sizes of the pumice and rock fragments found in deposits at various distances from the crater.[10]

The immense power of such an eruption has in modern times become a significant hazard to aviation. As recently as 1 October 1994, the Endeavor Space Shuttle viewed a spectacular eruption cloud from the Kliuchevskoi Volcano in the Russian Kamchatka Peninsula, which shot ash and gas over twenty kilometres (over 65,000 feet) into the atmosphere, but the hazards were perhaps most vividly illustrated by the case of a Boeing 747 airliner (KLM Flight 867) on 15 December 1989. This aircraft flew into the ash cloud of the Redoubt Volcano, located to the south-west of Anchorage (in Alaska), the airliner's destination. It had started to erupt some ten hours earlier and was 241 kilometres (about 150 miles) away from the airliner's position. Choked with ash, all four engines stopped working. After dropping more than 4,450 metres (14,600 feet) in a glide descent lasting five tense minutes, the crew managed to re-start the engines and land at their destination.

Vesuvius' explosion formed the cloud which Pliny memorably compared with the umbrella pine trees so common in the region (see Plate V). This cloud – a high, static column of gases and volcanic materials – contained pumice and ash that was carried downwind by prevailing winds from the north-west, and which gradually fell to the ground in order of weight, forming layers of pumice that decreased with distance from the crater. The first phase of pumice consisted of phonolitic magma (white pumice), which may have begun falling upon Pompeii roughly thirty minutes after the initial eruption, and continued into the early evening.[11] During this phase of the eruption, the pumice was not being deposited too heavily, perhaps at a rate of about fifteen centimetres an hour, but it built up inexorably, exerting pressure upon the roofs of houses until finally these gave way under the cumulative weight. Given that the typical house roofs were of a sloping design, it is likely that pumice accumulated more quickly in some

40

places, at twenty-five to thirty centimetres per hour, so that roofs began to collapse after about six hours.[12] Fragments of tiles and bricks from collapsed buildings have been found towards the top of this initial layer of pumice (although their presence in some cases may have been caused by the subsequent surge rather than by the pumice fall).[13]

The fall of pumice itself was probably not life-threatening, given the material's low density, although the consequences of a person being struck by a denser, larger fragment of old volcanic rock ripped from the inner walls of the volcano might have been fatal. These fragments, however, were much rarer.[14] Nevertheless, it has been calculated that about 400 victims were found in the initial layers of pumice, some of whom were killed by falling masonry rather than by the pumice itself. One body was discovered beneath part of the portico that had collapsed in the Large Palaestra, II.vii.[15] Another body, found under a column that had toppled down in the Forum beside the Temple of Jupiter, suggested to the nineteenth-century novelist Bulwer-Lytton a fitting end for his wicked priest of Isis, Arbaces.[16] People would have been able to attempt to escape, therefore, but it would have been difficult, given the unevenness of the surface under-foot due to earth tremors and the build-up of pumice, not to mention the artificial darkness created by the eruption which inspired Bulwer-Lytton to invent a memorable conclusion to his novel *The Last Days of Pompeii*.[17] Even further away, at Stabiae, we gain an impression from Pliny's account of the difficulties faced by people trying to flee:

> The buildings were being rocked by frequent strong tremors, and appeared almost to have come loose from their foundations and to be sliding this way and that. Outside, in turn, the falling pumice stones, though light and porous, caused fear, but this danger was chosen when compared with the others.... They placed pillows on top of their heads and tied them on with bits of cloth, as protection against falling objects. Now it was daylight elsewhere; there it was night, blacker and denser than any night, though many torches and various lights broke it up.
>
> *Letters* 6.16.15-17.

After white pumice had been falling for several hours, probably at an ever increasingly dense rate, the next stage in the eruption was marked by a change to tephritic phonolite, or grey pumice.[18] Following this, it seems that there was a moment of relative quiet during the eruption, in the early hours of the 25 August. Recent excavations at Pompeii (in the area of the 'House of the Chaste Lovers', IX.xii.6-7) have identified for the

41

first time a layer of grey ash and pisolites (pea-like rounded grains of limestone) between the pumice layer of the 'Plinian' phase and the first surge layer. This is what suggests the intervention of a period of time between the eruption's two main phases.[19] At this stage, it appears, people decided to venture out into the streets, only to find their way barred by the accumulation of pumice. This was the danger that had persuaded the friends of Pliny the Elder to awaken him at Stabiae: 'The courtyard from which his room was accessed had so risen by being filled up with the mixture of ash and pumice stones, that, if he had spent any more time in his bedroom, his way out would have been blocked' (*Letters* 6.16.14). The discovery of lanterns near bodies, and tunnels and holes cut through the walls of houses, are as likely to belong to these temporary survivors of the eruption as to explorers returning to the site at some later date. The lull should not have been welcomed, however, since it merely heralded the fact that the volcano was about to embark upon its most violent period of activity, a sequence of six pyroclastic surges and flows. These can be detected on the ground where thin layers of ash interrupt the grey pumice.[20]

Each sequence of pyroclastic activity consisted of two distinct components – a surge and a flow – different in character, but perhaps only seconds apart. The exact relationship of these phenomena is still disputed since, not surprisingly, it is not easy to measure this sort of rapid destructive force with accuracy. But, essentially, the first stage consisted of the ground surge, a 'highly turbulent current of hot gas and volcanic debris, which hugs the ground and precedes the pyroclastic flow at a very high speed'. This would have streamed down the slopes of the volcano in a billowing cloud at up to 200 kilometres (just under 125 miles) per hour, and at temperatures of 100°C, or higher. The surge carried with it only a low density of solid particles, whereas the pyroclastic flow that followed soon afterwards contained a high concentration of solid particles, a 'dense flow of hot fragmented volcanic material, lubricated by trapped gas and air'.[21] This flow proceeded in a different manner from the surge, also hugging the ground, but carrying larger rock fragments and pumice transformed into a liquid-like flow by tremendous heat. As a result, its direction tended to be channelled along by the natural topography and by the pattern of streets and buildings in the town. It advanced rather more slowly than the surge: speeds of sixty-five to eighty kilometres per hour have been calculated from the new excavations.[22]

In eruptions from modern times too, the ground surge leaves behind only a thin layer of ash, sometimes only twenty to thirty centimetres deep, and yet its destructive force is awe-inspiring: in the eruption of Mount Pelée, the surge caused sixteen steamships to capsize in the harbour of St Pierre, it wrecked masonry walls that were one metre thick, and its impetus propelled a three-ton statue of the Virgin Mary over a distance of twelve metres (almost forty feet) from its pedestal.[23] Likewise, the blast from Mount St Helens treated tall mature trees like matchsticks, flattening an entire pine forest for kilometres around. It is thought that these awesome forces are caused by changes in the nature of the eruption.

One hypothesis for the Vesuvian eruption is that the continuing eruption was accompanied by explosions occurring at ever deeper levels within the volcano. This resulted in a threefold decrease: in the gas content, in the height of the eruptive column, and in the level of violence. At the same time, however, the same quantity of material was being ejected. As a result of this combination of factors, the column partially collapsed and an avalanche of red-hot volcanic debris and gases veered off down the sides of the volcano.[24] This occurred six times (see Plate VI).

Herculaneum, only five kilometres (about three miles) from the crater to the west, was overwhelmed by the first such surge that occurred, in the early hours of the 25 August. By contrast to Pompeii, only a relatively thin layer of pumice (twenty centimetres) overlay the ground surface of Herculaneum, because of the direction of the prevailing winds.[25] In the past, the burial of Herculaneum under twenty metres of solidified material has been explained as the consequence of mudslides. It was thought that heavy rains followed the eruption, causing the deposits of ash and pumice upon the volcano's slopes to become detached and to slide down on top of the town. In this way, Herculaneum's burial was ascribed to secondary phenomena, rather than to the volcanic eruption itself.[26] It was also believed that, as a consequence, the town's inhabitants had been granted sufficient time in which to escape. Herculaneum's fate, therefore, has often been contrasted with that of Pompeii – the former being buried by mud, the latter by pumice and ash. In fact, however, it is likely that the fates of the two towns were more similar than has been appreciated, and that both were devastated by pyroclastic surges and flows. The solidified deposits that sealed Herculaneum so much more effectively than Pompeii are believed to represent six different surges that swooped down upon the town with devastating impact. Such was the violent impetus of these surges that they penetrated for several metres into the sea itself. Furthermore, recent excavations on the ancient harbour-front have revealed that by no means all the inhabitants did escape. By 1987, 139 bodies had been discovered crowded together within the boat-houses along the harbour-front, and doubtless many more await excavation. Careful analysis of how the bodies were found reveals that death must have been instantaneous – some people were even found sitting up, standing, or lying down naturally when the blast from the surge must have overcome them.[27] These excavations have given a clear picture of the violent force at work on inanimate objects too: a substantial marble basin in the hot-room (*caldarium*) of the 'Suburban Baths' was found to have been hurled across the room by the surge rushing in through the window (see Plate VII). Tiny pieces of window-glass were found implanted in the basin. Just outside the same baths, a life-size marble statue was severely damaged by the eruption process. The statue itself was propelled about fifteen metres (almost fifty feet) from its base, and the head of the honorand, Nonius Balbus, was discovered several metres from his body.[28] This now also helps to account for the confusion of early excavation reports, in particular in the theatre area, where bronze statues must have been toppled from their bases, and sometimes shattered into pieces (eventually suffering indifferent restoration work at the hands of eighteenth-century craftsmen). Finally, the ubiquitous presence in Herculaneum of carbonised wood and charcoal, which, it has been argued, was generated at a temperature of around 400°C, provides support for the new interpretation.[29]

The first two surges from the volcano (Surges 1-2) failed to reach Pompeii, stopping short at Oplontis and Boscoreale. A few hours later it was daybreak on the 25 August, but no rays of sunlight penetrated the darkness that enveloped Pompeii. At this point, a more powerful third surge did extend to the northern parts of the town. This surge (Surge 3) demolished parts of the town's walls, so that the subsequent flow proceeded unimpeded beyond this one, into the inhabited area.[30] The denser part of the flow was channelled along the streets, carrying along with it debris, such as tiles, bricks, and beams. Layers of deposits left by the flow are less dense in the town than in the surrounding countryside because of the interruption of buildings. The less dense parts of the flow charged over the tops of the houses, and continued on for tens of kilometres beyond the town, even over the Lattari mountains, disgorging ash.[31] Careful examination of the archaeological evidence reveals that Pompeii was devastated by three further super-heated avalanches (Surges 4-6) in short succession during the early morning hours. It has been estimated that the fourth surge, penetrating deep into Pompeii, killed about 650 people in the town. Consequently, most bodies have been found in the upper part of the pumice layer, in between the thin deposits produced by Surges 4 and 5. Their burial was then completed by the deeper layer formed by Surge 6, and by the final fall of pumice.[32] Recent work in the area of the 'House of the Chaste Lovers' (IX.xii.6-7) has identified a thin ash layer on top of the initial layer of pumice, representing the volcano's fourth surge, which sealed the end of the 'Plinian' phase of the eruption. In turn the fifth surge extended further south, and finally the most severe surge, Surge 6, at about 8 am, covered Pompeii with 90-110 centimetres (roughly 35-43 inches) of material, knocking down the walls of the highest buildings, and then proceeded as far as Stabiae.[33]

Vesuvius' victims would have been asphyxiated by the hot gases contained in the dust-laden cloud, which would have covered the distance from the crater to Pompeii in a mere six minutes.[34] At this point, there was no chance of escape. Those who had taken shelter inside buildings and who had awaited a lull in the eruption before venturing forth would have suffered a speedy demise. This pattern of human and volcanic activity is reflected in the distribution of the find-spots of bodies (Figs 5 and 6).[35] About 650 bodies have been found in the layers of ash resulting from the surges, and 394 bodies in the initial pumice layer. Far more of the former category of bodies than those found in the pumice layer were discovered in the streets, open spaces, and near the town's gates. Many of these victims were also heading in a southerly direction, away from the volcano. In general, bodies in the pumice layer, by contrast, have tended to be found within private buildings. Ironically, it is the layer of fine ash left by the surge covering the bodies that has been the archaeologist's best friend in allowing casts to be made of the bodies that reveal fine details, such as the chain collar which prevented a dog from escaping. The casts of the bodies of these victims, such as the thirteen adults and children discovered in 1961 in the 'Garden of the Fugitives' (I.xxi.2), remain some of the most moving sights to be seen at Pompeii today (see Plate VIII). It was not the fall of pumice that claimed these victims, but the violence of the pyroclastic surge. Similarly ironic is the protective capacity of the pumice that fell during the eruption: it was the very build-up of pumice that protected the lower sections of buildings in the town from violent destruction by the surge and flow processes, so that what we see today on site are the parts actually protected by the earlier phase in the eruption. By contrast, the parts of the buildings still protruding above the pumice were subsequently subjected to the full force of the surges. The last stage in the eruption

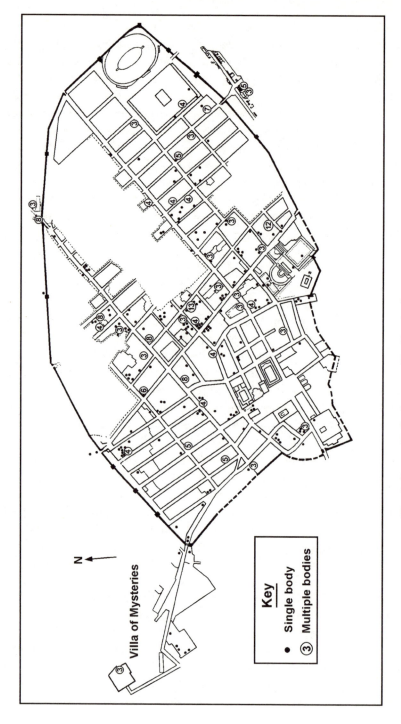

Fig. 5. Pompeii: find-spots of bodies in the pumice layer.

Key

- Single body
- ③ Multiple bodies

Villa of Mysteries

N

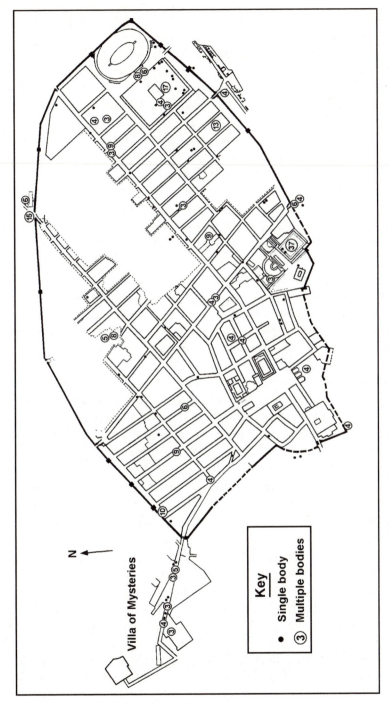

Fig. 6. Pompeii: find-spots of bodies in the ash layer, in streets and in open spaces.

consisted of a final explosion that deposited a layer of 60-70 centimetres (about 23-27 inches) of fine ash above the ground surge layers at Pompeii.

The destructive force of the eruption should warn against expecting too neat an arrangement of objects. A particularly gruesome illustration of this has recently come to light: in an alley off the 'Street of Abundance', next to the 'House of the Chaste Lovers' (IX.xii.6-7), the skeleton of a victim of the ground surge has been shattered by the force of the subsequent flow, since the body lay across its path. Man-made materials, such as tiles and bricks, being hurtled along by the flow, together with its load of volcanic debris, must have sliced off the parts of the body which had not yet been completely covered over by deposits, leaving behind only its right side in the place where the victim had died. As a result, the skeleton lacks its left arm and leg, and half of its skull. Its left foot, however, remained because it was up against a wall, where the layers of debris had built up a little more, protecting it. Another skeleton in this area had also suffered violence, its backbone being broken in several places, and its skull smashed.[36] Intensive research at this same locality in Pompeii, which had been previously unexcavated, has provided a much more complex picture of the impact of the eruption upon the formation of the archaeological record. In addition to noting down the exact layer in which an object has come to rest, it is now appreciated that an assessment has also to be made of the comparative vulnerability of the object towards disturbance in the eruption, and of the actual type of eruptive force that affected it, whether surge, flow, or earthquake.[37] The various phases of the eruption had their own characteristics, and impacted upon the fabric of the town in different ways.

In all, just over one thousand bodies have been identified at Pompeii over the years, a figure which may represent about a tenth of the town's total population. Even taking into account the likelihood that significant numbers of victims may have remained un-noted in the archaeological record, there seems a good chance that a good proportion of the town's population may have escaped to safety. Indeed, given the new reconstructed sequence of events, had the inhabitants started to flee as the first pumice and ash fell upon the town, they would have had time to cover some kilometres. Nevertheless, it would only have been feasible to try to escape on foot or by animal, and the obvious direction to take would have been away from the volcano, heading to the south, but this was also downwind of the eruption, and so progress would have been continually hampered by the volcano's fallout. The grim possibility also remains that people may have paused to gather together belongings, and may not have been able to flee very fast in the confusion caused by the combination of darkness, falling pumice and ash, and earth tremors. Forty-eight victims, some with jewellery, which they may have been trying to salvage, were discovered beyond the town's walls, in the direction of the ancient harbour.[38] As Pliny's letter reveals clearly, a strong northerly wind made escape by sea impossible at the time. It is sadly all too likely that hundreds, perhaps even thousands, of the volcano's victims still lie buried in the countryside just beyond the town's walls.

Haraldur Sigurdsson ends his recent account of the eruption with the following reflection: 'The cities of Vesuvius were now wiped from the face of the Earth and buried to a depth beyond the reach of excavation by the Romans. The deposit over Herculaneum was up to 23 m thick, and Pompeii lay under a blanket of 4 m of pumice. Gradually the memory of the cities faded into oblivion, until their rediscovery in the eighteenth century.'[39] Although more accurate of Herculaneum, this common impression misses out an important episode in the history of Pompeii – the period when the town was slumbering before being officially reawakened – as our next chapter will reveal.

3. A Broken Sleep

Titus: Romans, the sole object of my vows is your love; but your love must not be so excessive that it should cause shame to you and to me. However, I do not refuse those offerings. I wish only to change their use. Listen: Vesuvius has now erupted, exceeding its usual threat, and fiery streams flow from its sources; it shook the cliffs, filled the surrounding fields and neighbouring towns with ruins. The desolate people are fleeing; but misery envelops those left by the fire. That gold must serve as an example of help to those afflicted.

W.A. Mozart, *La Clemenza di Tito*, libretto to Act 1, no. 5

What happened in the aftermath of the eruption? Did the towns of Pompeii and Herculaneum fade from people's memories, buried out of sight? Such a disaster today would incite a global response, with governments and charities sending in relief teams to help the homeless re-establish themselves, and offering financial aid to rebuild the local communities. As the opera libretto quoted above shows, the Neapolitan-born librettist Metastasio had no doubts about how the good emperor Titus would have reacted to the disaster. No survivors of the catastrophe have left us written accounts of how they coped with their changed circumstances. Presumably some emigrated to new areas, but others may have wanted to stay in the localities known to them.

One individual who may have moved away from Pompeii in the aftermath of the eruption is recorded on a funerary inscription in northern Spain. This inscription is now lost, but is recorded as belonging to a grave-marker, or *stele*, showing a military relief. If it is not a modern forgery, this inscription is the tombstone of one Numerius Popidius Celsinus, a name known to us at Pompeii (and mentioned earlier in this book) as belonging to the six-year old boy who rebuilt the Temple of Isis during the town's last period of existence.[1] The tombstone's text reads: 'To the shades of Numerius Popidius Celsinus, town councillor ("decurion"), well-deserving. Quintus Cecilius his son set this up.' This combination of names – the first name Numerius, together with the family name Popidius – is certainly Pompeian in origin. Of course, this tombstone may not belong to the same youth whose early promotion to the town council is recorded at Pompeii, and who would have been in his late teens in 79, but may commemorate another member of his family. Nor is it proof that he emigrated only after the eruption. Nevertheless, this curious inscription raises the possibility that one survivor of the eruption may have been fortunate enough to have established himself in a new community.

Other than this, a poem of Statius (writing shortly after the eruption, in the reign of Domitian) congratulates a friend on the birth of his third child in terms that imply that Julius Menecrates had lost another family member in the eruption: 'Behold, now a third child increases the family of illustrious Menecrates. A noble crowd of princes grows for you and consoles you for the losses caused by mad Vesuvius' (Statius, *Silvae* 4.8.3-5). Given that Menecrates was the son-in-law of Pollio Felix, whose villa on the Sorrentine promontory is eulogised by Statius in another poem, and that he was, like Statius, from Naples himself, it is plausible that his family may have suffered some human loss in 79.[2] Such morsels of evidence hint at two possible responses to the disaster by those living in the region.

Even after the initial fallout from the eruption, there is some dispute about the extent to which life resumed some semblance of normality in the region. This issue involves two separate questions: first, whether or not people returned to the site of the catastrophe to salvage what they could, and secondly, the extent to which the area came to be repopulated, and when. Whereas Herculaneum was thoroughly sealed down by the huge depth of volcanic debris that had descended upon it, Pompeii was more shallowly buried. Although the region's topography was drastically altered by the eruption, notably the coastline and the course of the River Sarno, it is clear that the buried cities remained alive in the collective memory. The name 'Pompeii', along with the names of other buried towns – Stabiae, Oplontis, and Herculaneum – appears correctly marked upon the Peutinger Table, a twelfth-century map. It is unlikely, though, that this reflects current geographical knowledge during the early mediaeval period since this map was based upon a late antique map, which, in turn, was derived from earlier sources, some probably pre-dating the eruption.[3] At some point, local knowledge of the precise location of Pompeii must have disappeared, even though the name 'Civita' was actually used for the area beneath which the town was buried. Consequently, the first 'official' excavators in the 1740s believed for some time that it was ancient Stabiae that they had rediscovered.

It is important to assess what sort of responses to Pompeii's fate were provoked both in the immediate aftermath of the eruption, and then throughout its period of burial until its official reawakening in the mid-eighteenth century. Physical interventions in the buried town impose limitations upon archaeology, and allow us to uncover a snapshot of a day in the life of a normal Roman town only with due regard for the problems presented by the archaeological data available to us. The idea that the town was sealed up in a time capsule by the eruption has been influential upon the popular imagination, encouraged by comments such as this one by Maiuri: 'You will find the city just as it was abandoned by the fugitives .... For this reason Pompeii is the best understood and the most beloved city of all the ancient world.'[4] As we saw in Chapter 1, the expectation of finding a normal town pursuing its life uninterruptedly may be thrown into doubt partly because of the disrupted conditions under which life at Pompeii was conducted during the last fifteen years or so of its existence, as repeated earth tremors rocked the town. Chapter 2 illustrated how the violence of the pyroclastic surges and flows during the eruption contributed further to the chaos in which the archaeological record was created. This third chapter will now explore how even once this disorderly archaeological picture had been formed, it was still further disturbed by interventions during the 1,669 years between the eruption and the start of 'official' excavations in 1748.

The famous letters written by the Younger Pliny to the historian Tacitus (6.16, 6.20), providing him with an eye-witness description of the eruption on which to base his account of the event in the *Histories*, emphasise that both men were primarily concerned with celebrating the bravery of Pliny's uncle, the Elder Pliny, who died attempting to rescue a friend from the eruption. Pliny opens his first letter with the following words:

> You ask me to write to you about my uncle's death, so that you may relate it more accurately to future generations. Thank you; for I realise that if his death is commemorated by you, it will be granted undying fame. For although he died a memorable death that will make him survive for ever, in a disaster affecting the most beautiful areas, involving people and cities, and although he himself has written many works of lasting value, nonetheless your immortal writing will do much to perpetuate his name. In my opinion, lucky are those to whom it has been granted by gift of the gods either to do something worth writing about or to write something worth reading, but luckiest of all are those with both gifts. My uncle will count as one of these, through his own books and yours.
>
> *Letters* 6.16.1-3

Whereas historians today would probably wish to document the social and economic effects of the eruption, Tacitus apparently intended to construct his account as a eulogy of a great man, something which suits his professed historical aims elsewhere. In fact, all that survives of Tacitus' treatment of the topic is a brief allusion in his swift-moving programmatic prologue to the work, where he speaks of 'ruined or buried cities on the most fertile shore of Campania' (*Histories* 1.2). Otherwise, this work is lost to us from the period of AD 70 onwards. We have probably not, however, lost too much, since it is unlikely that it would answer the type of questions we might like to pose.

Two ancient writers – Cassius Dio and Suetonius – both mention a scheme established by the emperor Titus in response to some of the economic problems created by the eruption.[5] In the words of his near-contemporary biographer Suetonius, 'Titus selected by lot some commissioners of consular rank for the task of restoring Campania; he designated the properties of those overwhelmed in the eruption of Vesuvius, who left no surviving heirs, for the restitution of the afflicted peoples.' The epitomiser of the third-century historian Dio implies that Titus himself initially went to Campania in order to help the stricken area, but had to return to Rome following a devastating fire there. Indeed, inscriptions in Naples and Sorrento commemorate the emperor's financial support in restoring public monuments.[6] Certainly, then, Titus sought to help survivors, but did his scheme involve actually digging down through the volcanic deposits in order to salvage valuable objects? Another possibility is that property belonging to Vesuvius' victims elsewhere in Campania may have been redistributed.

It is far from uncommon for modern excavators to come across tunnels leading from house to house and large holes cut into the walls of houses.[7] These holes have sometimes been interpreted as evidence for the return of survivors soon after the eruption, who dug down beneath the volcanic material in order to salvage what they could of their own property, and that of others. A curious inscription suggests that some degree of co-ordination may have taken place. The Latin words for 'tunnelled house' (*domus pertusa*) in Greek letters were scratched upon the 'House of N. Popidius Priscus' (VII.ii.20), presumably left as a message that the house in question had already been explored.[8] Even this, though, does not provide unequivocal evidence for a systematic approach by Titus' commissioners to recovering property from the town, but may have been the result of unofficial co-ordination among individuals. One might even wonder whether or not tunnelling in the immediate aftermath of the eruption may have been motivated by the hope of recovering survivors as well as property.

In the early nineteenth century, the then director of the excavations, Carlo Bonucci, sought to make a strong case for the return of salvagers to the site, alluding to the 'authority' of an ancient inscription, which, he claimed, recorded that the third-century emperor Alexander Severus had plundered the site for marble, columns, and statues.[9] He did not directly quote from the inscription, but referred his readers to a more modern 'authority', the eighteenth-century German art historian, Johann Joachim Winckelmann. In his famous open letter to M. le Comte de Brühl of 1762, Winckelmann had linked the clear signs of earlier tunnelling found by contemporary excavators at Herculaneum with an inscription recording the transferral of statues 'from remote places' (*ex abditis locis*) to decorate baths of Severus. He deduced from this that statues from Herculaneum had been removed from the still buried town to decorate some public baths in Naples; a wonderfully romantic notion, but no more than that. Rather, the inscription is typical of late antiquity, and is similar to examples from elsewhere in Italy and North Africa, which commemorate the moving around of statues in late antique settlements by the local authorities keen to maintain the beauty of their towns.[10]

As always, however, the evidence is somewhat equivocal. In particular, it is often not possible to date the formation of the holes and tunnels. At least some of the damage can be attributed to inhabitants of the town at the time of the eruption itself. As we saw in Chapter 2, it is now believed that there was a lull in the eruption during the early hours of 25 August, when those who had taken refuge inside houses during the first phase of the eruption as pumice was falling, decided to make their escape. By this point, however, many found that their way was now blocked by pumice, so that they had to try to escape by digging their way out. The 'House of the Menander' (I.x.4) provides a likely instance of this scenario. Next to a large hole in the rear wall of room 19, three skeletons were found along with a pickaxe and drag-hoe. Maiuri suggested that they were attempting to reach a group of people trapped with their lantern in a nearby corridor; but they had failed to penetrate right through the wall before the pyroclastic surge overwhelmed them. The presence of the bodies of women and children elsewhere in the *insula* also supports the idea that these were victims of the eruption, rather than unlucky survivors who perished on their return.[11]

Although many of the tunnels in Pompeii probably do represent the vain attempt to escape by victims of Vesuvius, other tunnels were undoubtedly created only some time after the eruption. This has been illustrated in recent excavations, where the structure of one tunnel, using compacted ash as its vault, indicates that it post-dates the eruption by some time.[12] Furthermore, small but significant quantities of objects which must post-date 79 have been found on the site. For example, late antique lamps, and pottery dating from the sixth to the sixteenth centuries have been discovered in the Suburban Baths just outside the 'Marine Gate'.[13] Two late antique clay lamps, one with a cross in a disk and leaves, and the other with a dolphin, were found in 1755-6 in the estate of Julia Felix (II.iv), but the archaeologists at that time were not paying much attention to stratigraphy, so we cannot be sure precisely when those lamps were lost. Nevertheless, another late lamp was found only in 1974, in a room on the north side of the *insula occidentalis*, part of the property of M. Fabius Rufus, a large building constructed on several levels. This fact may be significant since the upper level of the building may have remained exposed above, or have been only just below, the eruption layers.[14] In this way, the late antique material raises the intriguing spectre of people much later choosing to dig down through the destruction layers in search of re-usable property, like the lead piping which was apparently removed at some point from the Sarno Baths (VIII.ii.17), leaving behind only a deep gouge in the wall.[15]

Of course, it is quite possible that the tunnels have no single explanation, but may represent the activities of all of these groups of people at different times. The cumulative weight of the evidence, however, points to the inherent unlikelihood that the town remained undisturbed from 79 down until the eighteenth century. Besides, now that archaeologists are looking more closely at the layers above that of 79, modern excavations have detected signs of disturbance to the stratigraphy, although it is difficult to pinpoint the period, or periods, when this occurred. For example, some parts of the complex around the tomb of the Lucretii Valentes at Scafati were found to have layers of ash, pumice, and earth all mixed up, in contrast to other parts where they remained perfectly sealed by the eruption, and this is a pattern which is found repeatedly in other digs within Pompeii.[16]

The eruption of Vesuvius was not forgotten in haste, but came to be used by writers to illustrate themes dear to their hearts. In the years immediately following the disaster, several poets commented upon the drastic change undergone by Campania, as for example in the following passage from Statius:

> These things I am singing to you, Marcellus, on the Cumaean shores, where Vesuvius revived its curbed anger, billowing forth fires to rival Etna's flames. Extraordinary to believe! Will future generations believe, when once more crops and these deserted places thrive again, that cities and peoples are buried below and that ancestral lands have disappeared, having shared in the same fate? Not yet does the mountain top cease to threaten death. May such a dreadful fate be far from your Teate, and may this madness not agitate the Marrucine mountains.
>
> *Silvae* 4.4.78-86

Elsewhere, in his eulogy to his deceased father, Statius describes how his father had intended to write an epic poem about the eruption (*Silvae* 5.3.205-8). Statius' own emotional involvement in the event was no doubt keener than that of other poets at Rome, given that his home town was Naples, and indeed several of the poems in his collection known as the *Silvae* celebrate locations in Campania. This is not to say, though, that other poets who lacked family connections with the area did not also draw inspiration from the event. Spanish-born Martial, for example, wrote the following epigram:

> Here is Vesuvius, just now covered with green shady vines; here the noble grape had squeezed out drenching pools; these the ridges, which Bacchus loved more than the hills of Nysa; on this mountain recently the Satyrs led their dances; this the home of Venus, more pleasing to her than Lacedaemon; this place was famous though Hercules' divinity. Everything lies submerged in flames and sad ash: nor would the gods above wish that this was allowed to them.
>
> *Epigram* 4.44

For other so-called 'Silver Latin' writers, whose works typically abound in violent subject-matter and style, the volcano provided them with a vivid image. Valerius Flaccus created two striking similes comparing the eruption with moments during battles in his epic, the *Argonautica* (3.208-10, 4.507-9), whereas Silius Italicus, in his epic poem on the struggles between Rome and Carthage in the Punic Wars, presented an eruption of Vesuvius as the culmination of a whole sequence of bad omens that had predicted disaster for the Romans on the battlefield at Cannae (8.653-5). This is not to say, though, that an eruption really occurred in 216 BC, but the recent disaster of AD 79 must have inspired this idea.

Later writers, too, continued to allude to the eruption. In arguing against his pagan detractors in the third century, the early Christian writer Tertullian stated that the lack of Christians at Pompeii at the time of the eruption proved that Christians could not be held responsible for all natural and military calamities, and so should not be punished for them (*Apology* 40). Another Christian, Bishop Pacian of Barcelona (St Pacian), in the second half of the fourth century, exhorted his congregation to repent of their sins. Rejecting traditional pagan accounts of torment in the Underworld for wrong-doers, like the feasting of the vulture upon the ever-regenerating liver of Tityus, he chose to represent the inexhaustible fires of Etna and Vesuvius as a fitting image of the hell-fires awaiting sinners who did not turn to penitence:

> Let no one believe in the liver of Tityus, nor in the vulture of the poets. ... Pay attention, if you do not believe it: when the soul will be in the fires deep down, it will be regenerated by a punishment that will also be its nourishment. ... Calculate the force of the torment from what one can already see: certain fumaroles consume huge mountains with subterranean fires. Sicilian Etna and Campanian Vesuvius seethe with untiring balls of fire: and so that they may prove to us the perpetuity of the judgement, they burst apart and are swallowed up, but they will not for all that disappear in centuries to come.[17]

This emphasis upon the continuing fires emitted by Vesuvius implies that his inspiration for this image may have come from more recent eruptions of the volcano, as much as from that of 79. For the more philosophically-minded, like emperor Marcus Aurelius (*Meditations* 4.48), the fate of Pompeii and Herculaneum merely provided another reminder that everything ends in death.

Some literary sources give the impression that life returned to normal quite soon after 79, but others emphasise the continuing desolation of the area. In the epigram quoted above (*Epigram* 4.44), Martial contrasted the past fertility of the slopes of Vesuvius with their present desolation, a theme which was echoed a few decades later by Tacitus too. In relating the emperor Tiberius' retreat to the island of Capri in AD 27, Tacitus provides a rare glimpse of his own contemporary world through the comment that 'Capri looked out over a most beautiful bay, before Mount Vesuvius erupted and changed the appearance of the place' (*Annals* 4.67). Another second-century AD writer, Florus, however, has seemed to some to suggest that the area soon flourished again, since he describes Vesuvius both as 'the most beautiful of all mountains' and as 'imitator of Etna's fire' (1.11.5). This part of his historical epitome of wars, however, narrates events of the 'Samnite War' many decades before 79, and so he is both depicting the volcano as he imagines it to have been before it erupted, and describing its character in his own day. Similarly, a poem of Statius (*Silvae* 3.5), which tends to be cited as evidence of regeneration around Vesuvius at an early date, should also be read as a literary construct rather than as a strict reflection of reality. So, when Statius played down the destruction inflicted by the volcano with the words 'Vesuvius' peak and the fiery storm of the dread mountain has not drained the terrified cities of their citizens so very much: the cities stand and are flourishing in their populations' (verses 72-4), he was not asserting that the buried cities had been revived, but that his wife should not worry too much about finding a suitable husband for her daughter outside Rome in Naples or Puteoli. Similarly, his assertion that Stabiae had been 'reborn' (verse 104) should be seen as part of his attempt to persuade his wife that the Bay of Naples would be just as pleasant a place of residence as Rome, with plenty to see and do, and the poet may perhaps be forgiven if he slightly exaggerated the situation.

Such apparent contradictions in literary representations of the impact of the eruption upon the region, then, are by no means irreconcilable, but can largely be explained by their context.[18] Of course, we may also turn to the evidence of archaeology in order to assess further the scope and chronology of the recovery of the area around the buried town. Photographs of the region devastated by Mount St Helens taken in the immediate aftermath of that eruption present us with almost a lunar landscape, a grey world deprived of all vegetation and habitation. The Vesuvian region must have presented a similarly bleak appearance for some time after 25 August 79. On the other hand, studies of the environmental impact of the eruption of Mount St Helens help to mitigate the bleakness of this picture to some extent. Even during the early autumn of 1980, just months after the eruption, new growth began to return to the region.[19] The speed of ecological rehabilitation varied according to the exact degree of damage in any given area: after seven years, six out of thirty-two resident small mammal species had returned to the areas worst affected, fifteen to the areas where trees had been blasted away, and twenty-two to areas which had suffered from falling tephra (the dust and rock fragments ejected by the volcano).[20] According to one estimate, the food chain in the area may be rebuilt completely over a period of about forty years.[21] It would be rash to draw a direct comparison between Mount St Helens and Vesuvius, not only because the two zones are so dissimilar ecologically, but also because it has been suggested that even the time of day at which an eruption occurs can make an impact upon the region's subsequent rate of recovery. Nevertheless, the example of Mount St Helens can at least be used to set up the hypothesis that the region around Vesuvius may have recovered significantly by *c.* AD 120, forty years after the eruption. This may then be tested against archaeological evidence.[22]

First of all, it should be noted that there is little evidence for the resumption of activity directly within the walls of the buried town. Later evidence generally falls beyond the boundaries of the Roman town. At the turn of the twentieth century, controversy was generated by finds to the north of the town, just outside the 'Vesuvian Gate'. In digging in this area, Antonio Sogliano believed that he had found the remains of a town built after 79. He uncovered some small masonry walls, which he believed to be foundations of buildings from the end of the first / early second centuries, which were later demolished and re-used for burials by the mid-second / third centuries AD.[23] Certainly the structures point to some sort of activity in that area after 79, but Sogliano went too far in interpreting them as a new Pompeii.

Nevertheless, recent interest in the question of the resumption of activity at Pompeii has led to the identification of a scattering of burials and structures in various areas, including via Lepanto in modern Pompei, and at Scafati (Fig. 7). A group of buildings in the area of via Lepanto provides the best evidence so far found for some resumption of life immediately around the buried town. This complex partly re-uses structures of a building buried by the eruption, and reflects habitation rather than burial.[24] Soundings carried out here in the late 1980s identified the substantial debris of building materials mixed in with pottery fragments. Some of the structures, including a basin with waterproof-concrete covering and lead piping, rest directly upon the ash layer deposited by the eruption in 79. Other evidence relates to later periods, namely the third and fourth centuries: walls belonging to housing and a workshop re-use the structures below them of a *villa rustica* destroyed in the eruption. Furthermore, a deposit of third / fourth-century ceramics probably represents a domestic rubbish heap. Four different soundings in the area brought to light many fragments of different types of pottery, including fineware, amphorae, and coarseware also dating from the third / fourth

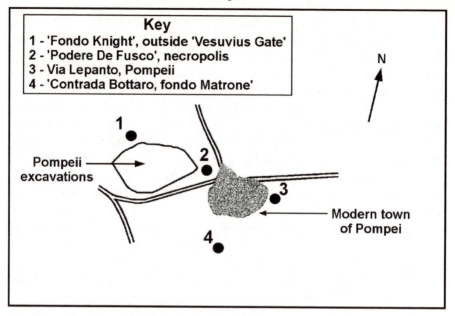

Key
1 - 'Fondo Knight', outside 'Vesuvius Gate'
2 - 'Podere De Fusco', necropolis
3 - Via Lepanto, Pompeii
4 - 'Contrada Bottaro, fondo Matrone'

N

1

Pompeii excavations

2

3

Modern town of Pompei

4

Fig. 7. Sites around Pompeii with archaeological evidence dating from after the eruption in AD 79.

centuries. From this, it seems likely that there was a small settlement in this area from at least the second century.

Generally, though, our evidence reveals small-scale non-monumental burials. For example, just outside Pompeii to the south-east, in 'podere De Fusco', a necropolis has been found, for which a fourth / fifth-century date has been posited.[25] The burials that are attested in the area are distinctly impoverished in scale – gone are the elaborate tomb monuments which the people of Pompeii had built for themselves in earlier times, replaced by simple burials inside *amphorae* or underneath tiles (known as 'cappucina' burials).

If we look at the area around Pompeii a little more widely, rather than at the actual site of the town, we can see signs of regeneration appearing in the second century. The Hadrianic period saw the rebuilding of the major road in the region. This road may actually have undergone emergency clearance soon after the eruption, but it seems to have waited a few years before being extensively reconstructed.[26] Its branch leading from Nocera to Stabiae was re-established in 121, and perhaps also the one from Stabiae to Naples. Three milestones, one from Naples, the other two from the road from Nocera to Stabiae, all display an inscription recording the road's repair at this date.[27] Although some action may have been taken soon after the eruption, a generation seems to have passed before normal transport could have resumed, when the essential infrastructure represented by the arterial road around the bay was fully repaired.[28]

Two fragments from necks of *amphorae* found recently in warehouses excavated in the south of France may provide new evidence for the resumption of large-scale viticulture in the Vesuvian area. These fragments belong to wine *amphorae* from a large group of *amphorae*, type Dressel 2-4, found at Saint-Romain-en-Gal (near Lyons) in second / third century deposits. They each preserve a painted inscription: 'SVR(rentinum vinum)', and 'GLABR(io) E[t]/ TORQ(uato) COSS.' The first inscription identifies the contents as 'Sorrentine wine' (almost the ancient equivalent of modern *lacrimae Christi* wine), while the second is a dating formula, recording the names of the consuls for AD 124. Analysis of the clay in the pots shows that it contains minerals that can be traced to the volcanic region around Vesuvius. This scrap of evidence might seem to suggest that by 124 the Vesuvian area had already recovered sufficiently to be exporting wine to the south of France, but much more work now needs to be done by pottery experts in looking for parallels for this type of *amphora* elsewhere before its significance can really be assessed.[29] Besides, it is also possible that wine production beyond the area affected by Vesuvius' pyroclastic activity may not have been disrupted much at all, particularly perhaps in the area of the Sorrentine peninsula, which must have suffered only from the earth tremors and the fall of pumice and ash in 79.

Overall, then, it seems likely that the area around Pompeii, and the Vesuvian region more widely, was beginning to recover by the AD 120s. This is ecologically plausible by comparison with the aftermath of Mount St Helens, and seems to be indicated by the admittedly meagre archaeological evidence. Sogliano's picture of the rebirth of a new Pompeii was based on an over-optimistic reading of the evidence, but he was certainly right to raise the issue of the resumption of life in the area. We should not forget, though, that further eruptions (in AD 203, 472, 505, 512 and 533) and earthquakes must have hindered large-scale redevelopment in the region. From a letter written in the early sixth century on behalf of the Ostrogothic King Theodoric by his chief minister Cassiodorus (*Miscellany*, 'Variae', 4.50), we learn that an assessment was to be made by the praetorian prefect regarding the remission of taxes and the extent of damage to territory around Nola and Naples following an eruption: 'The Campanians, devastated by the hostility of Mount Vesuvius, have shed abundant tears in begging for our mercy, asking that, given that they have been stripped of the fruits of their fields, they may be relieved from the burden of taxation.' The letter continues with a description of the impact of the eruption on the environment, and agrees to some form of tax relief, but ends with the concern of avoiding potentially fraudulent claims to exemption. In this way we are provided with a detailed snapshot of the continuing problems posed by Vesuvius for its neighbours.

Moving on to more modern times, we encounter a new episode in the history of the slumbering town with the construction of an aqueduct between Sarno and Torre Annunziata at the very end of the sixteenth century. For most of its route, it proceeded above ground, but some parts of it went underground, including a section lasting about 1,600 metres, beneath the hill known as Civita. This part of the aqueduct cut through the centre of the still buried town. Remains of the channel can be seen today in the south of the town, just before arriving at the 'Nucerian Gate' (see Plate IX). Its course can be retraced as follows: the north-west part of II.v; the 'House of Loreius Tiburtinus', II.ii.2; 'Nucerian street' between II.ix and I.xiv; 'House of the arches', I.xvii.4; 'House of the Menander', I.x.4; 'Stabian street' alongside the 'Temple of Zeus Meilichios'; northern section of the Triangular Forum; 'alley of the red walls', VIII.v.37; 'sanctuary of the Public Lares' in the Forum; northern part of the Forum. Contemporary documents record that the engineers discovered that they were digging through structures, discovering coins and inscriptions along their way. Two inscriptions found at that time included a dedication to Jupiter and a building-inscription set up by a local benefactor.[30] The local name of 'Civita' for the area became only too clearly illustrated.

By the end of the sixteenth century, then, we have definite records of the site being disturbed, but a literary masterpiece written about a hundred years earlier illustrates how Pompeii had been part of a locally inspired picture of Arcadia. The Neapolitan poet Jacopo Sannazaro composed his classically inspired work, *Arcadia*, in two phases, with the complete version being published in 1504.[31] In 'Prosa 12', the narrator has a dream from which he 'wakes up', goes for a walk, and is guided by a local nymph to various sights. In the course of this tour, he relates how they come into view of Pompeii:

But this town which we see in front of us is without doubt a city once famous in your country, called Pompeii, which was irrigated by the waters of the chilly Sarno. It was swallowed up by a sudden earthquake ... and now with these words we were very close to the city, which she was talking about, of which we could see the towers and houses, the theatres and the temples as if they were intact.

It would be fascinating to know whether or not this poetic vision was in any way based upon reality. Sannazaro was certainly well acquainted with the physical remains of antiquity in the Naples area, and had acted as official guide for visitors to the Phlegraean Fields, for example escorting the French ambassador around the ruins in December 1489.[32] Another of his works, *Rime Disperse* V, was a sonnet inspired by the ruins of Cumae.[33] Nor was this the only work in which Sannazaro drew upon local history. In the fourth *Piscatory Eclogue*, dedicated to King Ferrante, the mythological figure of Proteus sings a history of the Bay of Naples, starting with the war of giants and gods, mentioning the foundation and destruction of Herculaneum and Pompeii, as well as recalling famous sites further north – Cumae, the Sibyl's cave and Lake Avernus – finally ending with King Federigo, the father of Ferrante.[34] The poet's aim was clearly to glorify the city of Naples through its history, implicitly privileging its ancient glories above the history of Spain, under whose sway the kingdom was then held. It is clear that Sannazaro, if anyone, would have been interested if any parts of Pompeii were emerging from the countryside at that time, but we can only speculate whether or not this really was the case.

Even once the channel had penetrated the site, Pompeii was still not officially excavated for about another 150 years, but it did not for that reason remain undisturbed. Indeed, the discoveries made during the digging of the channel had led the antiquarian Lucas Holstenius to propose in 1637 the correct location for Pompeii, but others did not accept his proposal.[35] Even the discovery of an inscription with the letters 'POMPEI' found in 'excavations' during 1689 was interpreted as referring to a villa of Pompey the Great rather than to the town of Pompeii.[36] Another scholar, Camillo Pellegrino, also identified Civita as Pompeii, but again his idea was dismissed, partly because the ancient town was believed to be buried under Torre Annunziata. By the mid-eighteenth century, it is clear that unofficial excavations were proceeding apace at Civita. In a letter dated 10 February 1748 – in other words, a month before the engineer Alcubierre started digging officially at the site – Martorelli described to Gori the discovery of wonderful pictures, columns, and mosaics.[37] Indeed, it is likely that it was the very ease with which objects were turning up at Civita that may have prompted in the first place the diversion of energy and resources from Herculaneum, where, by contrast, conditions for excavation were so much more difficult and hazardous.

Long before the mid-eighteenth century, then, people were certainly well aware of the ruins lying under Civita. The prospect of Sannazaro having actually seen parts of Pompeii at the end of the fifteenth century gains some plausibility from a consideration of some of the comments made by eighteenth-century visitors to the site. Winckelmann, for example, observed in 1762 that the remains of Pompeii's amphitheatre had always been visible above ground.[38] Even more valuable information comes in an early description of a visit to the ruins of Pompeii, by François Latapie in 1776. He pointed out that, although official excavations had begun only recently, the locals must have long been discovering parts of the town when digging ditches to plant their vines. As he walked between the two main parts of the site excavated at that time – the Theatre and the 'Street of Tombs' outside the 'Herculaneum Gate', he described the countryside above the, as yet, unexcavated remains (see Plate X):

> In order to go to this other extremity of the town, which is towards the west, one crosses a land planted with vines supported by poplars, with lupins growing in between, which provide fodder for cattle here. This ground covers all the buildings of Pompeii as far as their top, but sufficiently lightly that one does not have to dig very far to uncover them. One even sees in some places ruins a foot above the surface of the ground.

He further suggested that cultivation and the re-use of materials for building houses and walls by locals had played some part in damaging the structures below.[39] By the time of this account, though, the period of the town's disturbed slumbers had drawn to an end, and its official reawakening had now begun.

I. Repair work on the
Building of Eumachia.

II. Inscribed marker set up
by Titus Suedius Clemens
outside the 'Nucerian Gate',
CIL X 1018.

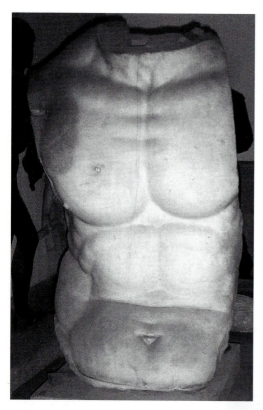

III. Torso of cult-statue of Jupiter, from Temple of Jupiter, NM inv. 6266.

IV. Rear side of torso, showing earlier relief.

V. An umbrella pine tree, with Vesuvius in the background.

VI. Cross-section through volcanic deposits from AD 79 eruption at Boscoreale, showing layers of pumice at the bottom, then surge and flow, and a petrified tree.

VII. Suburban Baths, Herculaneum: marble basin and its imprint in the lava.

VIII. Casts of bodies in the 'Garden of the Fugitives' (I.xxi.2).

IX. Channel of Sarno aqueduct near the 'Nucerian Gate'.

X. Unexcavated part of the site today.

XI. Statue of Charles Bourbon at Lucca.

XII. Bust of Giuseppe Fiorelli, Naples Museum.

XIII. Garden painting with basin, 'House of Marine Venus' (II.iii.3).

XIV. Central panel depicting Venus, 'House of Marine Venus' (II.iii.3).

XV. Plaster cast of plane tree root cavity next to Amphitheatre.

XVI. Plaster casts of vine root and stake next to replanted vine, in Villa Regina, Boscoreale.

XVII. Peristyle garden of the 'House of the Vettii' (VI.xv.1).

XVIII. Fishponds in the 'Estate of Julia Felix' (II.iv).

XIX. Wagon and tools in the 'House of the Menander' (I.x.4).

XX. Replanted vineyard (II.v).

4. The Reawakening

I am obliged to hide the name of the skilful artist who sent me these drawings for fear of attracting disgust upon him; because antiquity in Naples is a state matter and it is with some sort of anxiety that I offer information on the monuments of this region. I am anxious about making access to them even more difficult; but given that the difficulties cannot be any greater, on reflection I feel that there is nothing to be done and that accordingly one can surrender oneself to the joy of the moment.

Comte de Caylus, 1759[1]

The site of Pompeii had long been the object of investigation by curious treasure-hunters, as the previous chapter has illustrated, but the year 1748 marked the official reawakening of the site by extensive excavations. This process began in 1748 not as the result of some new acquisition of knowledge or awareness of what lay beneath the ground, but largely as the result of the political circumstances of that time.

In 1734, Charles of Bourbon won a decisive battle against the Austrians, and thus acceded (as Charles VII) to the throne of the Kingdom of the Two Sicilies, a large territory extending from Sicily itself, up through Southern Italy, to Naples, and beyond to the borders with the Roman States. For the first time in two hundred years, Naples became an autonomous kingdom, free from the direct rule of both Spain and Austria. The new kingdom did not gain universal acceptance at once, however: France did recognise it in May 1734, although it sent no ambassador, but the Papal States refused to acknowledge Charles' rule for several years, and it was not until 1741 that Savoyard Piedmont sent its ambassador. Furthermore, given that Charles himself was aged only eighteen, he was in reality not entirely free from the Spanish court's influence, even though he was nominally independent of the realm of his father, Philip V.[2]

It was during this period of uncertainty that Charles did his utmost to establish his new kingdom as one worthy of international recognition. The development of an impressive array of cultural institutions was no small part of this. A flourishing court culture could help to legitimate a new kingdom: the dominance of Naples by short-term foreign viceroys had left this aspect of political life relatively undeveloped, although not entirely neglected. In the seventeenth century, for example, the viceroy Don Alfonso Pimental had carried out excavations in the Phlegraean Fields, the volcanic area to the north of Naples, which yielded some statues to decorate the Palazzo degli Studi (now the Naples National Museum).[3] Naples had also already become recognised as an international centre for opera, with four conservatories and the appointment of Alessandro Scarlatti as the viceroy's 'maestro di capella' from 1684 to 1702.[4] Besides, the promotion of a culture distinctive to his court must have seemed an attractive way for the young king to assert his own independence from his parents at the court of Madrid.[5]

Right from the start of his reign in 1734, before either of the Vesuvian cities featured in his cultural and political strategy, Charles appears to have been partly inspired by his great-grandfather, Louis XIV of France, the so-called 'Sun King', who had dazzled Europe by his promotion of the arts and his construction of the magnificent palace at Versailles.[6] As Louis XIV had established by his patronage of Jean-Baptiste Lully during the 1670s and 1680s, and by his inauguration of the Académie d'Opéra, opera was important for any self-respecting dynasty. As noted earlier, Naples had already become a renowned centre for opera, but Charles promoted performances of opera still further. His new opera house, the Teatro San Carlo, was initiated in 1737, and completed within only a few months. This opera house was as much a place for the display of royal magnificence as for the performance of opera. The royal box was linked directly to the palace via a gallery, and the other boxes were held by royal permission only. In this way it became the venue for court-sponsored 'opera seria', a genre which during the eighteenth century sometimes even came to be called 'Neapolitan opera', so vigorously did it flourish there.[7] The glittering image of Versailles, together with his obsession with hunting, also prompted Charles to commission the construction of three new palaces, at Portici and at Capodimonte in 1738, and at Caserta a little later in 1751. Portici was on the doorstep of the excavations at Herculaneum, which Prince d'Elboeuf had briefly started from 1711, and which Charles continued from 1738, and the palace housed the ever-expanding collection of antiquities from the site. Capodimonte was on a highpoint overlooking Naples itself, and it too came to display the antiquities and pictures of the Farnese collection. Caserta, the rival of Versailles, a country residence designed by Luigi Vanvitelli, sixteen miles to the north-east of the capital, was by far the most ambitious project and was not completed until over twenty years later.[8]

In 1738, Charles married the daughter of the Saxon Elector, Maria Amalia. In emulation of her father's prestigious production of Meissen porcelain at his Dresden court, Charles founded a soft-paste porcelain factory in the grounds of his palace at Capodimonte. Although the porcelain designs chiefly depicted scenes from Neapolitan life, some also reproduced artistic treasures from Pompeii and Herculaneum, such as the famous equestrian statues of the Nonii Balbi, the father and son who had been major benefactors at Herculaneum, which graced the forecourt of Portici palace.[9] Marcello Venuti, the author of one of the earliest books on Herculaneum in 1748, also became Director of the porcelain works.[10] In 1781-2, some years after Charles had left Naples to become King of Spain, a whole set of porcelain with designs from Herculaneum was commissioned as a gift for him, as a reminder of the finds.[11]

Despite Charles' best endeavours, however, Naples was still an inferior cultural capital when compared with other Italian cities. At this time, Rome was the main centre of artistic treasures from the Roman world, with Florence following close behind. At first, Charles considered having copies made of many of the portrait busts in the Capitoline Museum at Rome, and was interested in buying collections rumoured to be unofficially for sale, such as those of the Este and Mattei families.[12] As it happened, however, one of the major collections at Rome, that of the Farnese family, which was displayed in the Palazzo Farnese, the Farnesina, the Orti Farnesiani, and the Villa Madama, was inherited by Charles from his mother, Elisabeth Farnese. Other parts of the Farnese collection were in Parma.[13] It was this latter collection that was transferred to Naples right at the start of Charles' reign, in 1735-9, to be eventually displayed in the Capodimonte palace. Such a transferral was not unusual for the times, given that collections of paintings and sculptures were comparatively mobile within noble circles, being sold off or offered as part of marriage settlements, but it does demonstrate clearly that Charles was already aware of the potential value of antiquities for increasing the prestige of his court.[14] The most famous artefacts in the Farnese collection, such as the Farnese Bull and Lysippus' Hercules, were in the Palazzo Farnese at Rome. According to the terms of the will of Cardinal Alexander Farnese of 1587, this collection was to remain in Rome in perpetuity.[15] This did not stop Charles from using the threat of removing the collection to Naples as a bargaining counter in his dealings with the Pope, although in the end it was his son, Ferdinand IV, who actually began to transfer it in 1786-8. This caused Goethe to lament in January 1787 that 'Rome faces a great artistic loss. The King of Naples is having the Farnese Hercules brought to his capital. All the artists are grieving'.[16]

By all of these means, Charles endeavoured to transform Naples, which was at the time the third most populous city in Europe, into a great cultural capital. Given that already by 1739-40 one well-travelled observer, Président Charles de Brosses, commented that Naples was the only town in Italy to have the character of a capital, it seems that Charles' efforts met with a great measure of success.[17] It is above all against the background of this feverish level of activity, whose aim was to transform Naples into a cultural showcase, that the excavations of Herculaneum and Pompeii should be viewed. The aim of the excavations was not primarily to gain knowledge about the past, but to gain prestige for the present, and it is this that overwhelmingly influenced the progress of the excavations throughout the rest of the eighteenth century.[18]

When his half-brother Ferdinand VI died in 1759, Charles relinquished the throne of Naples in order to return to Spain as Charles III. At this time his son, Ferdinand IV, was only a minor, eight years old, so a regency was set up, dominated by Marchese Bernardo Tanucci, formerly a professor in law at Pisa University. Consequently, Tanucci was to play a key role in the exploration and control of Pompeii over the next few years. Even as Ferdinand grew up, it became clear that he was no intellectual, being primarily interested in hunting, and that he showed little sign of excitement at the excavations on his doorstep. Nevertheless, he was urged by others to recognise the potential prestige to be gained from promoting the exploration of antiquity. In 1769, the Hapsburg Emperor Joseph II visited Pompeii with Ferdinand and took the opportunity to encourage the King to take more interest in the dig: 'Having found a spot where they were just digging up some pots and antique vases, he seemed to take infinite pleasure in it and was amused. I did not fail to encourage this inclination and explain all the advantages and prestige connected with it. He expressed a wish to return there more often and ordered the director to advise him whenever there were new discoveries.'[19]

Along with Herculaneum, Pompeii lays claim to being the birthplace of modern archaeology. To us, looking back on the earliest excavations, the investigations seem lacking in rigour and system, but it is perhaps unnecessarily harsh to judge eighteenth-century excavations by today's standards. At the same time, it is not only modern scholars who criticise the Bourbon era at Pompeii. Some contemporary observers too found fault with the excavations, most famously the art historian Winckelmann in his open letter on Herculaneum to M. le Comte de Brühl, which was swiftly translated into French and English.[20] Some of their sentiments chime in with today's, such as the criticism by Scipione Maffei that less impressive objects were simply being thrown away.[21] Sir William Hamilton, the British ambassador to Naples from 1764 to 1800, who closely observed both excavations and eruptions, wrote in a letter to Henry Temple, Lord Palmerston, on 19 August 1766 that he had suggested to Tanucci that the excavations at Pompeii should be carried out in a more systematic way. He deplored the current practice with the following words: 'Could one think it possible that, after the principal gate into Pompeii has been discovered at least five years, that instead of entering there and going on clearing the streets they have been dipping here and there in search of antiquities and by that means destroyed many curious monuments and clogged up others with the rubbish.'[22] On the other hand, a common criticism – that the pace of excavation was too slow and that instead the whole town should be uncovered within only a few years – seems rather naive to us. In 1776 François Latapie not only criticised the practice of digging at random points in the site, but also protested against the slow speed of excavation, commenting that only about one-tenth of the funds designated for use by the King for the dig was actually being used, that only about thirty men were actively engaged on site, and finally that the directors were negligent, ignorant and stupid.[23] Even Winckelmann lamented the fact that several generations to come would be left with something to excavate, given the slow pace of digging.[24] Nowadays, we are only too grateful that the Bourbons did not dig up the entire site.

The aim of the excavations at Pompeii was the recovery of artistic treasures for the royal collection. This explains the different attitude demonstrated by the Bourbon rulers to the excavation and publication of their antiquities from that shown elsewhere in Italy, notably on the part of the Vatican. Whereas, for example, the Pope claimed just one-third of all antiquities excavated in his domains and was willing to grant export licences for other finds, a royal edict in Naples claimed that all antiquities discovered in the Kingdom belonged to the King.[25] Furthermore, whereas other Italian states promoted tourism and encouraged foreign visitors to view, and even to collect antiquities, the Bourbon regime cloaked its new discoveries in a veil of secrecy. This was particularly marked in Charles' reign. Given that the excavations at Herculaneum remained deep underground, accessible only via tunnels and shafts, it was not too difficult to control who was allowed to visit them. Pompeii, though, presented a rather different prospect since there the digging was potentially visible to all. One early response to this was to cover areas over again once they had been explored and plundered for treasures. This was the fate both of the 'Estate of Julia Felix' (II.iv) and of the Amphitheatre, which had to be re-excavated later on. It is symptomatic of this whole approach that no classical scholar was employed on either the dig or in the Museum at Portici. Engineers such as Karl Weber and Joachim Alcubierre took charge of the digging, and the Museum was directed by Camillo Paderni, a sculptor and artist.[26] Furthermore, this overriding concern for finding *objets d'art* governed the pattern of digging: for example, as soon as it seemed clear that Pompeii's Amphitheatre was unlikely to yield sculptural treasures, digging there was suspended. Similarly, from 1751 to 1754, as the 'Villa of the Papyri' was being discovered at Herculaneum with its hoard of bronze statues and papyri, Pompeii remained neglected in order to concentrate on the more promising location.[27]

Once impressive finds started to emerge, great care was taken to ensure that the Bourbon court alone was associated with them and derived prestige from them. From 1738 the most impressive finds from Herculaneum, and later from Pompeii too, were displayed in the 'Museo Ercolanese' within Portici palace. The rarity of the objects on display there was guaranteed by the deliberate destruction of paintings not chosen for the Museum.[28] Similarly, only the best preserved (or rather, the most restored) bronze horse from the Theatre at Herculaneum was put on display: the others were melted down in 1770 in order to create a statue, candelabra, and other ornaments for the royal chapel at Portici.[29] Distinguished visitors, such as a diplomat from the court of Catherine II of Russia, Baron de Krüdener, in 1786, were allowed to view the collection, but they were closely guarded to prevent them from making drawings or taking notes, and were hardly given enough time to look closely at the exhibits.[30] In 1756, the Abbé Barthélemy commented in frustration after visiting Portici that 'one is only allowed to look, and one returns to Naples, with empty notebooks and a full memory'.[31] Even Goethe commented with surprise that 'We entered the museum well recommended and were well received. But even so, we were not permitted to sketch anything.'[32] Furthermore, given the emphasis on creating an impressive display rather than on presenting the artefacts in their historical context, the collection was organised thematically, with the result that, as Latapie observed, objects from Herculaneum and Pompeii were mixed together, with no record being kept of their original provenance.[33] Despite all these problems, however, Charles should at least be commended for leaving behind the collection when he returned to Spain, and not regarding it as a personal trophy.[34]

Publishing the finds was entrusted solely to the Royal Herculaneum Academy, founded by Tanucci in 1755. This institution had fifteen members, including the distinguished epigrapher Mazzocchi (whose participation in the project, however, involved composing pseudo-classical inscriptions in honour of the Bourbons rather than explaining ancient ones), and produced nine volumes of *Le Antichità di Ercolano esposte* (*The Antiquities of Herculaneum Displayed*) between 1757 and 1796. These lavishly illustrated volumes presented various categories of finds, including paintings and bronzes, and consisted of a brief commentary on each object, together with an engraving of it. The opening words of the foreword to the first volume left the reader in no doubt as to Charles' role as dedicatee:

In offering to your Majesty the first volume of the Antiquities of Herculaneum and its surrounds relating to a small number of the pictures, we are greatly honoured by your gracious kindness. Everything which we bring to you is already yours: yours is that same authority, which your Majesty grants us, to make them that which your Majesty himself has considered, decided upon, and then carried out at royal expense, with the greatest care, the highest taste, with fatherly love for our homeland, of such a degree and quality that makes you unique among all the sovereigns to whom our homeland has been subject.[35]

The foreword continues by observing that Europe can now witness the success of Charles' reign 'in creating a nation, which worthily is classed among the most cultivated by its military achievements, by its arts, by trade, by cleanliness, and by splendour'. Opposite this foreword is a large engraving carrying Charles' portrait within a medallion, underneath which military weapons on one side balance archaeological tools on the other.[36] These magnificent tomes were printed and distributed only as gifts to the select few, princes and famous scholars (including the Abbé Barthélemy and the Comte de Caylus): Sir William Hamilton's suggestion to Tanucci that money for the excavations could be raised by selling copies of the books initially fell on deaf ears. That would have defeated the whole aim of producing such an exclusive, limited edition. Only in 1770 were the volumes made available for sale at the cost of 16,000 ducats apiece.[37]

The point that the Kingdom's antiquities were solely at the disposal of its rulers was further strengthened by the commissioning of multiple copies of portraits of the royal family as gifts for other European rulers, some of which depicted them visiting the sites and transporting antiquities.[38] Sometimes, however, the Bourbon rulers seem to have adopted an amazingly casual attitude towards finds if they were not unique in themselves. Ferdinand even parted with eighteen Herculaneum papyri in exchange for eighteen kangaroos in order to provide exotic animals for the menagerie of the Villa Floridiana, the residence of his mistress, the Duchess of Floridia.[39] After all, how were eighteen from a total of 1,805 going to be missed? At any rate, visitors to Naples were left in no doubt about the exclusive rights of the Bourbons over the excavations, as the doctor John Moore, accompanying the son of the Duchess of Argyle, commented in 1782: 'They dig only to hunt down treasures. If the King's attention were less fixated on valuable objects, the city would by now be completely uncovered.'[40]

Despite the fact that the Bourbon regime sought in this way to make the new discoveries accessible only to a select few, news of the sites gradually filtered through Europe, attracting visitors to Naples. At first, Pompeii was almost dismissed by some, as far inferior in richness to Herculaneum. De la Roque reported the opinion that the lack of valuable antiquities being uncovered there was thought hardly to compensate for the expense of the excavations: 'Pompeii, which was much less considerable and much less rich than Herculaneum, up to this day only offers few antiquities of a certain merit; hardly (people said to us) offsetting the expenses caused by this research.'[41] Nor was this sense of disappointment limited to visitors: the excavators too felt frustration at the lack of progress. In a letter to Charles III on 9 December 1760, Tanucci reported on Alcubierre's impatience at Pompeii: 'At Civita, there are trifles – nails and glass – some pieces of glass, bone, and terracotta. Don Rocco is impatient at the barrenness of this excavation.'[42] Nevertheless, the much easier conditions for digging and the lack of a modern settlement on top of the site, in contrast to Herculaneum, persuaded the excavators to continue digging, even though Pompeii was much less impressive than Herculaneum. Given these sentiments, it is no surprise that the rhythm of excavations at Pompeii was far from even. In 1748-9, the Amphitheatre, the street of tombs outside the 'Herculaneum Gate', and some houses were investigated, but interest waned during 1751-4, when the 'Villa of Papyri' at Herculaneum was given top priority. Furthermore, even after more interest in Pompeii was shown from the 1760s, as Tanucci and La Vega planned to uncover the Theatre district, the devastating famine which afflicted Naples in 1764, killing 40,000, cut off funds from the excavations for a while. Indeed, the Abbé Coyer remarked at the time that the authorities should be praised rather than criticised for the slow pace of excavation, given the severe hardships being suffered by the populace of Naples.[43]

In many respects, Pompeii was a disappointment: no statues to rival canonical classics, like the Apollo Belvedere or the Laocoon, were being found. Nor did Pompeii match up to the current ideas of Roman antiquity, which had been conceived from ancient literature and the grand architectural monuments at Rome. Roman civilisation had not been imagined as existing on an everyday level.[44] In his description of his visit to the site on 11 March 1787, for example, Goethe expressed surprise at the small dimensions of the town's buildings:

> Everyone is astonished by the small, cramped size of Pompeii. Narrow streets, although straight and provided with stone walkways on the side; little windowless houses, the rooms that lead from the courtyards and galleries lit only through their doors. Even public works, the bench at the gate, the temple, and then also a nearby villa are more like models and doll's houses than buildings.[45]

Similarly, de la Roque commented that 'All the rooms there are small and badly lit, even in the grander houses.'[46] On the other hand, in common with other eighteenth-century visitors, de la Roque was impressed by the discovery of window glass in a villa just outside Pompeii, given that it was not all that common in contemporary domestic architecture. Of course, in time, it was exactly this difference between Pompeii and Rome – the way in which mundane artefacts and aspects of everyday life were revealed – that captured visitors' imaginations. Charles Dickens' account of his visit to Pompeii in 1844 in *Pictures from Italy*, for example, shows how he was particularly struck by 'the little familiar tokens of human habitation and every-day pursuits', such as 'the chafing of the bucket-rope in the stone rim of the exhausted well' and 'the track of carriage-wheels in the pavement of the street'.[47] These, of course, are often the features of the site which today's tourists remember most vividly, but back in the mid-eighteenth century, Pompeii initially failed to live up to the expectations already created by Herculaneum. Even so, Pompeii soon seemed to compensate for the initial disappointment by delivering up so many paintings, since Roman wall paintings had previously been known only from a very few examples, such as the 'Aldobrandini Wedding' (now in the Vatican).

The discovery of the Temple of Isis in 1764, with its paintings, statuettes, and bodies, helped to revive interest in Pompeii. Not least, the immediacy of its finds – including the remains of a meal, and bodies identified as being those of the priests – attracted attention. In addition, its rarity as an 'Egyptian' temple in Italy prompted curiosity.[48] Even so, visitors were initially rather disappointed at the temple's lack of splendour: in 1769, the mathematician and astronomer Joseph Lalande noted that the temple was rather unimpressive, lacking attractive marble facing, instead having brick columns faced with stucco, describing it as

> a small temple, totally intact except for its roof, but which gives only the slightest idea of this town. The columns are of brick covered with stucco; there are some very mediocre sculptures. The walls were covered with frescoes which have been detached for taking to the King's museum. The staircase that leads to the sanctuary is narrow, clad with white marble with greenish veins, and which is less fine than Carrara marble.

In the 1786 edition of his work, however, Lalande was more enthusiastic about the temple, describing it as 'the most curious part of these antiquities', and revising his negative view of its architecture: 'The style of this architecture is pleasing rather than severe, the orders are in small proportions.' He now also commented much more on the possibilities for reconstructing the activities in the temple from the utensils, paintings, and bodies found there.[49] This change of heart reflected the growing enthusiasm for the temple among its visitors: for example, in 1784, Gustav III of Sweden commissioned Giovanni Altieri to make a cork model of it as a souvenir of his visit, and in 1785, King Ferdinand commissioned some porcelain on Egyptian themes as a gift for the Duchess of Parma.[50] Similarly, an illustration showing a fantastical reconstruction of religious rites in the temple published in *Voyage Pittoresque* by the Abbé de Saint-Non in 1777 reflected the fascination evoked by the temple and its cult.[51]

Once news of the discoveries had spread through Europe, Naples became a compulsory stop on what became known as 'the Grand Tour'. This expression is primarily valid as a description of the European tours made by young noble Englishmen (and some Scotsmen too), and it should be noted that the 'Voyage d'Italie' and 'Italienische Reise' of tourists from France and Germany created a greater diversity of visitors and responses to the site.[52] For example, several French travellers who made accounts of their journeys were bourgeois in background rather than aristocratic. Charles-Nicolas Cochin was in charge of the royal coin collection from 1753 and travelled at the state's expense in order to enlarge this collection. Some French visitors were also rather older than the typical Grand Tourist from England, being over forty. A number of them – including Cochin, Président Charles de Brosses, the Abbé de Saint-Non, and Joseph Lalande – sent reports to the large academies in Paris, such as the Académie des Inscriptions et Belles-Lettres or the Académie de Peinture et de Sculpture, and some were also correspondents of other large European academies, such as the Royal Society of Antiquaries in London.[53] Nevertheless, their descriptions were not necessarily works of professional scholarship and might even repeat whole passages from other accounts. By contrast, other Grand Tourists, such as Baron de Krüdener, who was writing about his journey for his mother at Riga, had quite different aims in producing their accounts.[54]

Many visitors found the volcano itself as fascinating as the site and the Museum at Portici, if not more so. During this period, Vesuvius was at its most active in modern times, starting with a large explosive eruption in 1631, with other eruptions following the accession of the Bourbons in 1737, 1751, 1754, 1760, 1767, 1774, 1779, 1786, and 1794. Many visitors climbed up the crater, sometimes even during an eruption, and many artists painted dramatic scenes of the erupting volcano. One of the richest men in France, Jacques-Onésyme Bergeret de Grancourt, commissioned Pierre-Jacques Volaire to paint an eruption by moonlight for his country residence, the Château de Nègrepelisse. Volaire's work was based upon his own observations of the volcano, and indeed he had accompanied de Grancourt on an excursion to the crater edge on 23 April 1774 while the volcano was actually erupting. De Grancourt recorded that he was particularly pleased with the way in which Volaire had succeeded in capturing the horror of Vesuvius.[55] Equally dramatic was another painting of an eruption by Joseph Wright of Derby, produced *c.* 1776-80, which is one of around twenty-seven such scenes. This time, artistic licence included Ischia and Procida in the scene, neither of which would in reality have been visible, in order to emphasise the contrast between the fury of the volcano and the calm sea. In addition, small figures in the foreground, whose dress could equally well evoke a classical or contemporary setting, are seen carrying away a victim.[56] By contrast, another landscape, by Jakob Philipp Hackert, *c.* 1774-5, concentrates upon representing a lava flow in a realistic fashion, and distances itself from the dramatic views provided by other artists.[57] Given too that there were so many restrictions upon painting scenes of the antiquities, one suspects that the volcano was welcomed as being a subject open to all.

In many ways, then, Vesuvius was a prime attraction, and visitors wanted a memento of the volcano as much as of the antique. The architect Sir John Soane, who visited in 1779, included in his collection 'a piece of cinder from Vesuvius' as well as a piece of painted wall plaster.[58] So greatly did the eruptions capture people's imagination that the Stuwer family in Vienna put on spectacular firework displays representing eruptions of Vesuvius.[59] This fascination continued well into the next century, and Charles Dickens was later to devote many pages to his account of his ascent of the snow-clad volcano, by far the liveliest episode in his description of the ruined cities.[60]

Of course, a visit to Pompeii remained a compulsory component of a Neapolitan tour, even if it sometimes seemed less exciting than climbing Vesuvius. Some such visits by Grand Tourists actually had an impact both upon the way in which Pompeii was being excavated and upon the ways in which it was being represented in art. On a basic level, it is clear that the most prestigious visitors to Pompeii were provided with a spectacle of digging. When the novelist Sir Walter Scott visited shortly before his death in 1832, an excavation was staged for him, although nothing much was forthcoming, only a few bells, hinges, and other everyday metal objects.[61] Care was sometimes taken to ensure that visitors would witness the discovery of something impressive, even if finds which had already been found had to be reburied and then 'found' for a second time in an orchestrated performance. For example, a fine bronze statue of Apollo found in 1811 in the 'House of Apollo' (VI.ii.22/15) was immediately reburied, only to be 'discovered' two days later in the presence of Queen Maria Carolina.[62] We also hear of visitors being invited to use a pickaxe themselves. Even the excavation notebooks recorded significant visits, such as the one by King Ferdinand and Emperor Joseph II mentioned earlier. An entry for 7 April 1769 records how they inspected the progress of digging in various parts of the site, including by the stage area of the Theatre, and how Joseph II kept questioning the way in which the excavations were proceeding, putting pressure on the King to increase the workforce.[63]

Even less distinguished visitors, however, might make their mark on the site by purchasing small finds to take home with them. Whereas today most people are content to settle for replicas, eighteenth-century Grand

Tourists took home the real thing. An ink drawing by Henry Tresham, *c.* 1790, depicts an archaeological dig which is unidentified, but which closely resembles a Pompeian house. Visitors are gathered around a table examining small finds, such as bronzes, vases, and lamps, while other finds are being brought to them by the excavators.[64] Occasionally, it is possible to trace the Pompeian origins of an artefact long since carried off abroad, such as a small inscribed altar in the Prussian collection of the Count of Dohna von Waldburg. Such artefacts are only reincorporated with difficulty into studies of Pompeii: this particular inscription, which reads 'To Augustan Isis. Manilia Chrysa', was omitted from the standard collection of monumental inscriptions from Pompeii, *Corpus Inscriptionum Latinarum* X.[65] Similarly, a marble statuette of Diana reported found in 1839 has disappeared without a trace, and may have been among finds given to the visiting Princess of Saxony.[66] We are unlikely ever to know just how many early finds disappeared in this way.

A number of letters from the Abbé Barthélemy to the Comte de Caylus in 1755-6 also reveal that visitors to Rome were not surprised to be offered paintings from Pompeii for sale. In the first letter in which he mentions such paintings (5 November 1755), the Abbé Barthélemy asks his friend to keep quiet about them, since, he says, M. de la Condamine wants to be the first to make such paintings known in France. This captures well the competitive atmosphere of the time. By 11 November 1755, the Abbé has himself bought one of the paintings, at great expense, and it is only much later, on 17 February 1756, that a letter from M. de la Condamine to the Comte de Caylus raises questions about their authenticity. As it turns out, the paintings actually appear to have been freshly composed by a painter in Rome, taking advantage, it seems, of the fact that the secrecy surrounding the excavations gave potential purchasers little chance to test their authenticity. Even so, the King of Naples bought the remaining paintings for his Museum, perhaps in the fear that even the circulation of forgeries purporting to come from Pompeii might undermine the exclusivity of his collection.[67] More skilled collectors, however, clearly managed to acquire real antiquities from Pompeii in spite of the high levels of security, as an account of a visit to Sir William Hamilton by Goethe further reveals. Goethe recounts how, as a trusted friend, he was allowed to see artworks stored in a secret vault:

> In a long box on the ground, with a loosened top that I inquisitively shoved aside, lay two quite magnificent bronze candelabra. I made a sign to get Hackert's attention, and asked him in a whisper whether these were not

similar to the ones in Portici. However, he made me a sign to keep silent; of course, they had probably found their way here obliquely from the Pompeian tombs. On account of these and similar fortunate acquisitions, the baronet may well have let only his most intimate friends see these hidden treasures.[68]

Despite the high level of secrecy surrounding Pompeii, some artists did succeed in producing pictures of the site, by stealth, by memory, or, presumably in cases where their patron was of sufficiently high status, by royal permission. An example of this last category is probably a portrait of Anna Amalia von Weimar, 1789, by Johann Heinrich Wilhelm Tischbein. This represents her seated on the tomb of the priestess Mamia, just outside the 'Herculaneum Gate'. She visited Italy in 1788 partly for reasons of health, but also inspired by Goethe's letters about his Italian journey. The painting is essentially a realistic representation of the tomb, although the layout of the inscription is altered to render the entire text legible, but the painter has also added theatrical masks in the background to reflect the sitter's role as a significant patron of the arts. In addition to taking this painting home with her, Anna Amalia also set up a copy of the tomb in her park at Weimar. In part, her royal status must have allowed such a direct representation of a monument at Pompeii as part of her portrait, but the artist's appointment as Director of the Neapolitan Academy of Painting may well have been an important factor too. At the time, Queen Maria Carolina had been promoting the interests of German and German-Swiss painters at her court, including Angelica Kauffmann and Jakob Philipp Hackert.[69]

Hackert painted a number of scenes of the ruins of Pompeii which, in common with his work as a whole, are distinguished by their realistic, almost photographic, character. Hackert's privileged place at court is revealed by some comments of Goethe, who describes him as 'the famous landscape painter, who enjoys the special confidence and most particular favour of the king and queen'. Hackert had been granted a wing of the Francavilla palace at Caserta as his residence. Goethe visited him there, noting both the special trust placed in him by the queen, who had asked him to instruct her daughters in art, and her pleasure in his company, delighting in discussing artistic matters. Once again, however, it seems likely that it was not just the artist's favour with the Bourbons, but also the importance of the individual who commissioned the work that resulted in permission to produce such scenes. Hackert's painting of the Theatre district of Pompeii (1799) was commissioned by Thomas Noel Hill, 2nd

Lord Berwick. It seems likely that this commission can best be understood against the political background, as Napoleon was advancing ever closer to Naples. In this case, Ferdinand IV's authorisation of the production of the painting may well have been prompted by his realisation that the British would become likely allies against Napoleon, and this was one way of winning support.[70]

In other cases, however, visitors were forced to adopt covert means in order to make their sketches of the ruins. Sir John Soane explained in his third lecture to the Royal Academy in 1810 that his drawings of the Temple of Isis 'were made from sketches made by stealth by moonlight, and are, I believe, accurate'. As has been pointed out, however, his belief was not entirely well founded![71]

The discovery, excavation, and publication of the antiquities of Pompeii and Herculaneum remained central to the image of Charles Bourbon for some generations to come. Although he was compelled to leave Naples at a relatively early stage in the excavations, it was Charles rather than Ferdinand who gained more prestige from the finds. Even after he had departed for Spain, the volumes of *Le Antichità di Ercolano* continued to be dedicated to him, and in an illustration symbolising his apotheosis by Charles Nicolas Cochin of 1777, the antiquities find their place among the commemoration of his achievements. The focal point of the picture is a medallion with Charles' portrait and the legend 'CAROLVS III PARENS OPTIMVS' ('Charles III, excellent father'), and other smaller medallions allude to his achievements. At the bottom right of the picture, a cherub is depicted holding an open book on which can be read 'Antiquités d'Hercu-lanum'.[72] Even much later, in 1822, his grand-daughter Maria Aloisia of Bourbon set up a statue of Charles suitably attired in a toga in Lucca in Tuscany (see Plate XI), with a Latin inscription stating that this action was designed 'in order to remember and protect her ancestral glory': in this way the prestige associated with the excavation of Pompeii continued to be exploited for generations to come.[73]

5. The Politics of Archaeology

If you would like to put all the newspaper writers, all the artists, painters, sculptors, and architects, in a state of ecstasy, you have but to issue a decree couched in these terms:-

'In the name of the artistic world, the excavations of Pompeii shall be resumed and continued without interruption, as soon as I reach Naples.

G. Garabaldi, dictator.'

Letter from Alexandre Dumas to
Giuseppe Garibaldi, 25 August 1860[1]

The inexorable advance of Napoleon Bonaparte's army through Europe in the last years of the eighteenth century sharply curtailed the number of visitors coming to Naples on their Grand Tour, and it was only after the Battle of Waterloo in 1815 that travellers began to swarm back once more. From 1796, the antiquities of the Kingdom of Naples had a part to play in soothing the strained relationship between Napoleon and Ferdinand IV. Alongside demands for financial settlements, the peace proposals of that year included the provision for Napoleon to lay claim to one hundred statues, pictures, or manuscripts from Naples, as well as the right to excavate at Pompeii, Herculaneum, and Portici. Nor was this the first time that Napoleon had sought to gain control of another realm's cultural treasures: not long before in similar circumstances, he had demanded five hundred manuscripts and a hundred art objects, to be chosen by French commissioners, from Pope Pius VI. Venice was even more unlucky: in 1797, the famous gilded bronze horses of St Mark's were simply seized as war booty and set up on a triumphal arch in the Tuileries in Paris. Following the short-lived Parthenopean Republic and Bourbon restoration in 1799, the state of uneasy truce between the Bourbon monarch and Napoleon prompted the French ambassador, Baron Alquier, to suggest further gifts as a sign of friendship in 1803. Alquier recommended sending a selection of antiquities from Herculaneum and Pompeii, including mosaics and frescoes, and various everyday utensils. He particularly coveted for his leader some of the papyri from Herculaneum, which the King had earlier refused to give to other sovereigns, eagerly suggesting that any results of

80

their successful decipherment in France would be reported back to Naples.[2]

Eventually, however, the French cat ceased to tease the Bourbon mouse, and Ferdinand IV (who became Ferdinand I of the Two Sicilies on his subsequent return) and Queen Maria Carolina were forced into exile in another part of their realm, Palermo, taking with them a selection of their most prized antiquities out of the reach of the French. On 8 February 1806, Joseph Bonaparte crossed the border as the new ruler of Naples, to be succeeded (on his departure for greater things in Spain) by Joachim Murat, the husband of Caroline Bonaparte, in September 1808. Joseph Bonaparte's enthusiasm for the site is suggested by the fact that he made his first formal visit there on 2 March 1806, less than a month after he had taken up his new position, but the brevity of his reign obviously imposed limits on the extent of his intervention at Pompeii.[3] By contrast, the Murats were in power long enough for their reign to mark a huge surge of interest in Pompeii, with the Queen visiting the site repeatedly and pouring in money to fund excavation. Indeed, she was said to have wanted to see the whole of Pompeii cleared within three or four years.[4] It was during this period that the daunting tasks of clearing the Amphitheatre (1813-16) and the Forum (from 1814) were undertaken. The Amphitheatre had actually been one of the first buildings tackled by the earliest Bourbon excavators in 1748, but they had abandoned the project as yielding too few results for the effort required.

Murat had never been over-excited at the prospect of ruling Naples, since he had expected, in the light of his success in winning the country for Napoleon, to become King of Spain. Consequently, he was not very happy when Napoleon offered him a choice between Naples or Portugal, and declared that he would not accept Portugal on any terms.[5] Naples seemed rather a minor realm when compared with other prospects, such as Poland and Switzerland, and in 1815 his ambitions seduced him into misguidedly marching northwards, in the hope of becoming King of United Italy. His defeat at the Battle of Tolentino (in The Marches, near Ancona) on 3 May marked the turning point in his fortunes, with the result that he was forced to depart from Naples for the last time on 19 May, leaving the way open for the return of the Bourbon dynasty from exile.[6]

The way the excavations at Pompeii were conducted from the 1820s was typical of the whole Bourbon government at that time. The historian Harold Acton describes how deeply corrupt practices pervaded the system: 'More than ever before gratuities – *regalie* – were typical of every government department, and the Neapolitan citizen became so inured to them that he regarded them as reasonable, fair and honest.'[7] At the same time, this period of Bourbon resurgence was vitiated by political unrest. The 1820s saw revolution and insurrection in Naples, which were brought under control only by the billeting there of the Austrian army until 1827. By the mid-1820s even the supporters of the 1820 revolution were beginning to regret their actions, given the expensive burden of the Austrian occupying forces.[8]

Although an immediate rush of visitors was only to be expected in 1815, as the Continent opened up again to the British in particular, what was perhaps less anticipated was the way in which the initial rush did not die away. Instead, travellers to Italy kept on increasing in number during the 1820s, 1830s, and even 1840s. Visitors began to return to Naples, with as many as 7,000 foreigners staying in Naples in 1837. As in the eighteenth century, these visitors included many distinguished royal personages. In honour of the visit of the Dowager Queen Adelaide of England in November 1838, parts of the site being excavated at that time were given their names ('House of Queen Adelaide of England', VII.xiv.5, 18, 19, and the 'Alley of the Queen's Excavation', running from north to south between VII.xiii and VII.xiv). But a new feature among the British was the presence of women, family groups, and members of the upper-middle class.[9] No longer was Italy primarily the destination of young noblemen. The 1830s also saw several changes in the provision of transportation, which encouraged greater numbers to make the journey into Italy. Napoleon's 'Grande Route Militaire' over the Simplon Pass was supplemented by the end of the 1830s by roads that could support wheeled traffic over the St Bernard, St Gotthard, and Brenner Passes, substantially decreasing the discomfort and dangers of crossing the Alps. During the same decade, a regular steamship service also began to run between Marseilles and Naples. Furthermore, Ferdinand II's encouragement of the construction of the first railway line in Italy, from Naples to Granatello in 1839, which was envisaged as only the first step in creating a long-distance link with northern Italy, also made the Kingdom more accessible to travellers within Italy itself.[10]

Despite a period of relative stability and prosperity in the 1830s, an uprising in 1844 sought to make Ferdinand the constitutional sovereign of a United Italy, and from then on, until the annexation of Naples to the kingdom of Italy in 1860, liberal unrest elsewhere in Italy spread into Naples and created a turbulent political background for the organisation of the excavations at Pompeii and the Museum in Naples.[11] It is precisely during this period, from 1843, that the career of one man, the Neapolitan-born Giuseppe Fiorelli (1823-96), began to be inextricably linked with the history of excavation at Pompeii (see Plate XII).

The name of Giuseppe Fiorelli is often associated with the rise of a more 'scientific' approach to archaeological exploration at Pompeii, and indeed it is no exaggeration to state that both the site of Pompeii and Naples Museum were totally transformed under his direction, the former from 1860 and the latter concurrently from 1863 until 1875. In many respects, however, his innovations can be viewed as largely representing pragmatic responses to problems, especially political ones, rather than springing from an awareness of the need to transform archaeology for its own sake. Furthermore, his reforms in Naples and Pompeii appear not to have sprung solely from his own ideas, but to have drawn upon earlier suggestions, notably proposals made in 1848-9. These proposals, to which we shall return later, were designed to bring some order and discipline to the excavation and administration of Pompeii. Admittedly, Fiorelli had played an important part in drawing up these proposals, but the likelihood of input from others, notably Raffaele d'Ambra who actually signed the report, should not be forgotten. So, do the changes at Pompeii and Naples reflect the contemporary political revolution rather than an archaeological one?

Fiorelli's early career was closely dependent upon personalities and politics in Naples.[12] His main interests at this stage were numismatics and law: he was not an archaeologist as such, but in this period archaeology was still not really a distinct discipline: for example, the excavations at Pompeii had always been directed by an engineer or architect. Fiorelli's first publication on coins, *Observations on some rare coins from Greek cities (Osservazioni sopra talune monete rare di città greche*, 1843), drew attention to this young scholar, only twenty years old, and resulted in his election as correspondent to various scholarly academies, including the Herculaneum Academy. Having finished his studies, he was appointed in 1844 to a post as an Inspector for the Superintendency in the coin-room of Naples Museum. In the following year he participated in the Seventh Congress of Italian Scientists in Naples, which King Ferdinand II sponsored in an attempt to show that he was not as narrow-minded as some of his liberal opponents claimed. Even at this early stage in his career, Fiorelli was not content to cherish the status quo, but attempted during this congress to make accessible the whole coin collection of the Museum.

Even though we do not know anything about Fiorelli's political sympathies at this time, it may be significant that in general the participants at the congress took the opportunity of such a gathering to debate political issues. Despite the fact that the King entertained them lavishly for two weeks, they persisted in pursuing their own agenda to such an extent that the Neapolitans dubbed them *scoscienziati* ('men without conscience') rather than *scienziati* ('scientists').[13] Fiorelli's self-defence of 1849, in which he protested that he had always been more inclined to the peaceful study of archaeology rather than to political activities and content 'to live more with the ancients than with my contemporaries', doubtless owed more to his concern to extricate himself from the political charges levelled at him at that time than to reality.[14] This contrasts markedly with the later tendency of his compatriots to paint him as a hero of the Risorgimento. For example, in his obituary notice for Fiorelli in 1896, Giulio De Petra claimed that it was because of Fiorelli's influence 'in inspiring him with feelings of liberty and Italianness' that the Count of Syracuse wrote in 1860 to his nephew, the King, urging him to abdicate, and to Victor Emmanuel, pledging his loyalty.[15]

In 1847, Fiorelli was transferred to Pompeii, as Inspector of the Royal Excavations at Pompeii, as a result of disagreement with the Museum's director, Francesco Maria Avellino, who was himself apparently becoming increasingly frustrated with the huge task of organising such a fast-growing collection. Even in the most propitious of circumstances, the sheer quantity of artefacts in the Museum and their unparalleled diversity would have created huge logistical problems for cataloguing, classifying, displaying and storing them. Furthermore, having taken over the direction of the Museum in 1839 from Michele Arditi, Avellino had inherited the problem that no attempt had been made to keep the Museum's inventory up to date for the previous decade. In 1842, Avellino had tried to create a forum for discussion among the scholars in Naples by founding one of the few archaeological journals in Italy, the *Neapolitan Archaeological Bulletin* (*Bullettino archeologico napoletano*), but this initiative had failed through lack of funds. By the end of 1847, Avellino sent a report to Minister Spinelli complaining of the chaos in the Museum, the result not least of the ill-educated, unscrupulous characters of its custodians.[16] On arriving at Pompeii, however, and on finding that malpractices had flourished there too since the Bourbon restoration, Fiorelli came into conflict with the site's Architect Director, Carlo Bonucci. Fiorelli criticised the lack of concern for the preservation of finds on site and the potential corruption made possible by the presence of a private house owned by one Dell'Aquila (whom he scathingly described as 'the real boss of the excavations') within the confines of the site.[17] He also condemned administrative irregularities, thefts and bribery, pointing the finger at Bonucci in particular. These criticisms not surprisingly gained him several enemies, who were soon to turn against him. Furthermore, because of the inseparability of archaeology from the royal court, Fiorelli's criticisms ran the risk of being not just academic observations, but of crossing the fine line between objective administrative criticism and criticism of the government, and by implication the King. It is difficult to judge, however, the extent to which Fiorelli himself was following a liberal agenda in making these criticisms. Certainly his friendship with prominent 'liberals' such as Mariano D'Ayala and Pasquale Stanislao Mancini may suggest that he was prompted to speak out against abuses for political as well as academic reasons.[18]

Ferdinand II's decree of 29 January 1848 granting a Constitution was widely celebrated in Naples, but euphoria soon gave way to anarchy. On 10 March, spurred on by the extremist Aurelio Saliceti and supported by the national guard, radical students took it upon themselves to expel Jesuits from Naples, while the chief of police and the government could only look on. At the same time, feelings were running high against Austria, with Saliceti demanding a declaration of war in pursuance of Italian independence. War was in fact declared on 7 April.[19] Fiorelli's response to this highly charged atmosphere had been to form a volunteer unit of the national guard from among the custodians of Pompeii.[20] On 10 March he had written a letter to the newspaper *Il Tempo*, declaring that, together with the custodians of Pompeii, he was ready to defend the Constitution with two cannons and a company of artillery, having sworn absolute loyalty to King Ferdinand. Fiorelli drew upon the past in order to support his position, claiming (erroneously) that Pompeii had never been defeated in the Social War against Rome. He summoned up images from archaeology to inspire others, with the declaration that a soldier had been found where he had died, standing guard at the 'Herculaneum Gate', having chosen death rather than desertion as his fate.[21]

Despite the distraction of foreign affairs, the domestic crisis deepened still more, as it became clear that the deputies were not prepared to take an oath of allegiance to the King and the Constitution at the opening of Parliament on 15 May. The sense of rebellion spread to the streets of Naples, where seventeen large and sixty-two small barricades were erected, leading to widespread bloodshed on 15 May, when troops were called in to disperse protestors.[22] It seems all the more remarkable that it was only a week before, on 8 May, that King Ferdinand II had established the Commission for the Reorganisation and Reform of the Bourbon Museum and the Ancient Excavations in the Kingdom, of which Fiorelli was the Secretary. At the same time, other major cultural institutions, such as the Royal Bourbon Library, were also designated for reform.[23] This commission drew up a far-reaching 'law' covering all aspects of archaeology, which was to reveal all too clearly the close relationship between politics and archaeology at the time.[24] As mentioned earlier, Fiorelli was a leading voice in drawing up these new regulations for the Museum and excavations. Some of the proposals attempted to combat the corruption and thefts which had been taking place, establishing a fixed code of conduct for the custodians, transferring elsewhere personnel known to be corrupt, and including penalties for omitting to report finds. The whole administrative structure at Pompeii was to be altered. The four Supervisors at Pompeii were to be properly qualified, and to hold their posts for two years only, and a new post of Inspector was to be introduced above that of Architect Director, a measure which was largely a response to the corrupt practices of Bonucci earlier. A programme for proper publication of the excavations, complete with pictures and plans, was also drawn up.

The proposals as a whole extended far into the academic community, suggesting that excavation should be incorporated into a teaching framework, with six professorships being established in Naples University, receiving stipends from the Museum. Furthermore, the Royal Herculaneum Academy was to lose many of its privileges, not least its monopoly in publishing finds from Pompeii, which was to devolve to a body of professional scholars, the Superintendency, including the six new professors. In future, official drawings of finds were to be delivered to the Superintendency, and not to the Academy. Had it ever been executed, this step would have decisively severed the royal Bourbon court's control and deprived it of this unique source of prestige. Another significant change in ideology is reflected in the first article proposed by the law, stating that the Museum's displays were to be for the benefit of all citizens. This marked a major shift away from the idea of a jealously guarded royal collection, open only to a select few on request. No longer was a special permit from the royal household to be necessary for a visit to Pompeii, although visitors were not to be allowed to wander around unattended. This new emphasis on accessibility extended to rules about publication: in future, anyone was to be allowed to draw objects on display, with the proviso that objects remained protected for the first four years. Even more radical was talk of the national ownership of some objects.[25] Finally, the suggestion was made to establish a museum at Pompeii itself, not as a challenge to Naples Museum, but in order to accommodate objects not wanted there, such as empty *amphorae* without inscriptions, everyday cooking wares, uninscribed lead piping, skeletons, perfume jars, and fragments of all sorts of metal and pottery.

The law was submitted to the Ministry on 3 November 1848. Had its recommendations been followed, the archaeology of Pompeii would have been transformed and the strong ties between archaeology and the royal court would have been seriously undermined. Indeed, the whole ideology behind the excavations would have been changed for the better, since the commission explicitly condemned the practice of treasure-hunting. But political tensions deepened, and the King disbanded the commission on 28 August 1849, with the result that the reforms proposed in the law were doomed.[26] Earlier in that same year, on 24 April, Fiorelli himself was arrested for political crimes against the King (including participation in the barricades, conspiracy and possession of illegal arms) and imprisoned. The extent of Fiorelli's actual involvement in political conspiracy at the time is unclear, but what is clear is that the swiftness of accusations made against him were largely due to the enemies he had made through his criticisms in Pompeii and Naples. In a letter that he wrote to the German archaeologist Henzen on 3 January 1849, Fiorelli reported that his accusers included Carlo Bonucci and Bernardo Quaranta (professor of archaeology and Greek literature at Naples University), whose positions of power Fiorelli had undermined with his criticisms.[27]

Fiorelli's enemies were powerful enough to secure him about ten months in prison, but even during this time he attempted to correct some of the deficiencies he had detected in Pompeian scholarship. During his imprisonment, he gathered together information on the excavation of Pompeii from contemporary documents produced since 1748. He clearly saw the importance of publishing contemporary accounts of the excavations. On release from prison in 1850, he published the first in a projected series of about eight volumes bringing together this invaluable material on the history of the excavations. By doing so, Fiorelli was deemed to have offended against the regulation that all publications dealing with the excavations needed official sanction. As a result, one of his arch-enemies, Quaranta, spurred on the authorities to search Fiorelli's house, seizing and burning the manuscripts found there, along with the printed book

itself, *Journal of the Excavations of Pompeii: Original Documents Published with Notes and Appendixes* (*Giornale degli scavi di Pompei: documenti
originali pubblicati con note e appendice*).[28] Fiorelli tried to find a publish-
er outside Naples, but without success, so this project had to await the
change in political climate in 1860 before being accomplished.[29] Although
effectively excluded from returning to any official public position in the
aftermath of his imprisonment, he acted as private secretary to Count
Leopold of Syracuse from 1853 to 1860, supervising his excavations in the
necropolis of Cumae and publishing in 1857 a volume on the painted pots
found there (*Notizia dei vasi dipinti rinvenuti a Cuma nel MDCCCLVI*).

What Fiorelli did manage to publish on Pompeii in this period set new
standards in accuracy.[30] His publication of the Oscan inscriptions from the
town of 1854 (*Monumenta epigraphica Pompeiana ad fidem archetyporum
expressa. Pars prima. Inscriptionum oscarum apographa*) contained large
illustrations, reproducing the form and colours of the letters by means of
the new technique of chromolithography (the art of printing colours from
stone).[31] This format was ahead of his time and set a new standard, which
was initially adopted also by the earliest volumes of Latin inscriptions in
the series *Corpus Inscriptionum Latinarum* (published from 1863).[32] As
the title of Fiorelli's book indicates (*pars prima*), it was envisaged as being
only the first in a comprehensive series publishing all the inscriptions from
Pompeii, but it actually remained the only one to be published.

Another innovation had more far-reaching effects: Fiorelli's publication
of an overall map of the excavations in 1858 (*Tabula Colonia Veneriae
Corneliae Pompeis*), dividing the town up into sections, became the basis
for all future work on Pompeii's topography (Fig. 8). The map was supplemented by a three-page article, 'On the regions of Pompeii and their
ancient distribution' ('Sulle regioni pompeiane e sulla loro antica distribuz-
ione'), which suggested how the urban development of Pompeii was
reflected in its physical layout.[33] His system of dividing the town up into
nine regions (*regiones*) and town-blocks (*insulae*), although subsequently
modified in its detailed arrangements given that his proposals for the
layout of the then unexcavated areas did not match what was later found
there, was to become the standard way of pinpointing a particular location
in the town. The value of his system is only too clear when compared with
the alternative system often adopted, of naming houses after their supposed proprietors or in honour of some contemporary figure or event. To
give a single example in full, the 'House of the Faun' (VI.xii.2, 5, 7) has also
been known at different times as 'House of Pan', 'House of Goethe', 'House

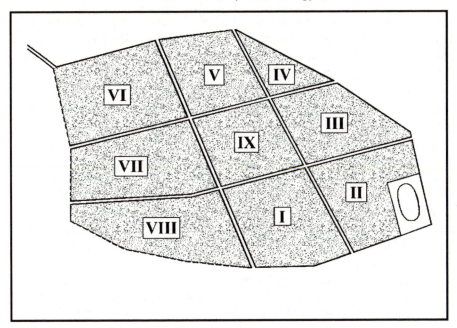

Fig. 8. Fiorelli's system of *regiones*.

of the Large Mosaic', 'House of the family of Purius Magius', 'House of Arbaces the Egyptian', 'House of the Battle of Alexander', 'House of M. Cassius', and 'House of the Lucretii Satrii'. Houses have often accumulated in this way a whole series of names, as their owners have been re-identified (for example with the 'House of Loreius Tiburtinus' becoming the 'House of Octavius Quartio', II.ii.2), or as the honorand faded in significance (the 'House of the Faun' being named as the 'House of Goethe' in honour of the famous writer's son who was present at its excavation in 1830, but who died of smallpox a few days later). Likewise, as political circumstances changed, so too could the names of Pompeian houses, with the 'House of Queen Caroline' (VIII.iii.14) being initially named in honour of the wife of Joachim Murat, then becoming the 'House of Adone' with the return of the Bourbons, only to revert to its original name once more after they were in turn deposed. As has been commented, 'the aura of venture in that French era of the early 1800s outlasted the pusillanimity of the Bourbons'.[34] Fiorelli himself was extremely cautious of such a habit, stating in his article that 'I have excluded any arbitrary naming, as many times as I have not succeeded in knowing for certain the real names of the owners of places'.

Garibaldi's victorious entry into Naples on 7 September 1860 ushered in a new era not just for the Kingdom, but also for the excavations and antiquities of the realm. At least, it did so after a brief false start. First of all, however, the great general committed a grave error of judgement, offending local sensibilities by appointing a foreigner as the honorary Director of the Museum and of Pompeii.[35] This was the Frenchman Alexandre Dumas, better known to us as the author of historical novels such as *The Three Musketeers* and *The Man in the Iron Mask*. In March 1860, Dumas had set out from Marseilles on a voyage to Greece and the Middle East, but by June he had sailed only as far as Alicata, when he decided to join Garibaldi. He was eager not just to witness an adventure which might have come from the pages of one of his novels, but also to participate actively in the conflict. He records his decision in his account called *The Garibaldians*:

> On leaving Girgenti, I quitted Sicily, with the intention of going direct to Malta, and from Malta to Corfu, but when I put into the little port of Alicata, to take in provisions, a feeling something like remorse caused me to change my plan. Why should I not be present, I reflected, at the close of this great drama of the resurrection of a people? Ought I not to do all in my power to aid it?[36]

His offer to Garibaldi in a letter of 21 June that he procure weapons from France met with a warm response from the general.[37] Dumas also bore a personal grudge against the Bourbons, in the belief that Ferdinand IV had poisoned his father in 1806, having imprisoned him in 1799. One might feel some scepticism about this claim, inasmuch as it required Dumas to believe that his father survived the poison for six years before succumbing. Dumas declared: 'Moreover there is another ground – a personal one, too – why I should feel particularly glad for Garibaldi to take Sicily. ... It happens that I am at war with the King of Sicily.'[38] His personal vendetta against the Bourbons was nothing new at this time: already in 1834, his name had appeared on a blacklist of those to be barred from entering the Kingdom, for fear that he would stir up revolutionaries, and he claimed that King Ferdinand had threatened him with serving in the galleys for four years if he were to set foot in Naples. As well as providing Garibaldi's forces with a thousand muskets and 550 rifles, he wrote fulsome accounts of Garibaldi's victories and acted as the general's ambassador.[39]

Consequently, Dumas evidently felt justified in asking for two rewards at the successful conclusion of the campaign, and requested charge of the excavations and Museum, as well as permission to hunt in the park of Capodimonte.[40] As the quotation at the head of this chapter indicates, Dumas had prepared the ground for this request, by urging Garibaldi already in August to announce that he would resume the excavations at Pompeii. Dumas was very enthusiastic about digging at Pompeii, and insisted that although he was happy not to take a salary, he did not want to be director in title only. In achieving this goal, however, he encountered some reluctance from Garibaldi: despite the fact that Dumas had carefully drafted an appropriately worded decree for Garibaldi to issue (cited at the start of this chapter), the actual decree of 15 September contained several changes, and Dumas' letter to Garibaldi on 16 September, protesting that 'I asked for a title without salary, but I did not ask for a sinecure', met with no response.[41]

Dumas' interest in the antiquities was no passing fancy, as he had devoted several chapters of his 1843 work describing his travels, *Le Corricolo*, to an account of his visit to Herculaneum, Pompeii, and Naples Museum in 1835.[42] In anticipation of his appointment, he had also already written to Paris to recruit scholars, archaeologists, engravers, and draughtsmen. His ambition was to produce an illustrated history, updated by the results of the excavations he intended to promote. He also intended to enlist the help of Victor Emmanuel, by asking for a company of sappers to help with the basic donkey-work.[43] The people of Naples were outraged at Dumas' appointment, and Garibaldi's extra concession, that Dumas should reside in the palace of Chiatamone, formerly belonging to Joachim and Caroline Murat, did nothing to alleviate their hostility. A newspaper article on 25 September protested at the appointment, stating that 'Italians feel it is a great scandal. It seems to them that a director of the Museums might have been found in Italy with much greater merit than this Frenchman.' Finally, Dumas himself lost heart when a popular demonstration against him, albeit of only three hundred men and lasting only a few minutes, chanted 'Out with the foreigner!' As related by one contemporary observer, Maxime Du Champ, Dumas was reduced to tears, lamenting: 'I was used to the ingratitude of France, but I did not expect it from Italy.'[44]

Dumas apparently had ambitious plans for what he wanted to achieve in Pompeii and at the Museum, which he published in detail in a pamphlet entitled 'Project for a National School of Painting, Sculpture, and Literature', and also in a series of articles in the *Indipendente* after he had been forced to resign. His political sympathies contributed to at least some of his plans for Pompeii, since he declared: 'I want to arrange the performance one day in the restored theatre of Pompeii of Aeschylus' *Prometheus*, and to applaud the first Titan fighting against the first Tyrant for the triumph of the same idea which 5,000 years later is victorious today.' He also drew Garibaldi's attention to the fact that some of the employees at Pompeii had not been paid for two months. Otherwise, two more of his plans are worth noting. First, he proposed that on next discovering a rich house, it should be restored to its state in AD 79, complete with its furniture, and that it should function as a local museum and educational resource for archaeologists, architects, and painters. Secondly, he suggested introducing some sort of entrance fee for visitors to the site, which would be used to support students of painting, architecture, and sculpture.[45] As we shall see later, this latter proposal foreshadows what Fiorelli actually implemented soon afterwards, although the eagerness to reconstruct a particularly splendid building was doomed to wait some years longer, because of the lack of funds. It is not impossible that Dumas' widely publicised plans for Pompeii, as well as the proposals made by the 1848 commission, may have influenced Fiorelli's later actions.

The subsequent advancement of the local Fiorelli must have seemed much more felicitous to the Neapolitans. In 1860 he was appointed as Inspector of the excavations of Pompeii and to a new chair of archaeology at Naples University, which he held until 1863 when he took over the direction of Naples Museum alongside that of the site of Pompeii, as its Superintendent.[46] He has generally been acclaimed for adopting more rigorous archaeological methods. He is probably best known for preserving the bodies of Vesuvius' victims by creating plaster casts of them. This was actually his second idea for dealing with the problem of the site's collection of bones: in 1848, he had suggested transferring skeletons to the Institute of Anatomy at the University, but the King had vetoed this idea.[47] In fact, Fiorelli was not the first to adopt this archaeological technique, but he did extend its use more widely.[48]

Once Fiorelli was installed as site director, a number of important reforms took place. A new system for recording the progress of the dig was introduced and the content of excavation daybooks was regulated. Some idea of the new regulations for drawing up the excavation diaries can be gained from a provisional description of them published in 1861.[49] This sets out how the diary is to be compiled by the Supervisors, and is to include details of the date, time at which the work started and ended, the number of workmen, the precise place of excavation, and the number and quality of objects and buildings found. An architect is to add his observations to this. Each record is to be numbered and stamped on every page by the Superintendent, and to be submitted to the Inspector of the excavations (i.e. Fiorelli himself). These directions reflect the way in which attitudes to publication were changing. In the eighteenth century, when the Royal Herculaneum Academy was solely in charge of publishing the results of the excavations, the lavish volumes of *The Antiquities of Herculaneum* (*Le Antichità di Ercolano*) had been designed as a glorification of the Bourbon king, and were not even initially commercially available, being distributed only as gifts. The end of the Bourbon kingdom resulted in the end of such regal books. Subsequent books inevitably lost their glamour, but gained in accessibility. Nor was it only style and presentation that changed, but also content.

Fiorelli's work marked a fundamental shift in approach to the antiquities of Pompeii: whereas discussion had previously been based around individual art objects and buildings, Fiorelli now sought to elucidate the overall history of the town. Up to that point, individual Pompeian paintings had attracted comment because of their representation of Greek myth; no interest was shown in their potential to illuminate Pompeian society, nor even in their artistic styles.[50] Furthermore, Fiorelli's work first acknowledged specifically that texts were of only limited use in reconstructing ancient history, and that archaeological evidence could be used extensively as an independent source, stating that textual sources are 'certainly not sufficient for reconstructing the history of Pompeii'.[51] These new aims were encapsulated in his publication of 1875, *Description of Pompeii* (*Descrizione di Pompei*). This was essentially a tour of the town, describing its state in AD 79, but containing a substantial introduction considering both archaeological and literary evidence for the site's earlier history. His overarching conception of the town was also physically represented in a different form of publication, namely the model on a scale of 1:100 depicting the whole of the site excavated up to 1861, which was subsequently updated to 1879.[52] This model complemented his earlier topographical work in publishing his 1858 map.

At the same time as ensuring more effective controls upon the publication of the results of excavation, Fiorelli also introduced a more systematic approach to excavation as a whole. Whereas previous excavations had been dotted about the site, Fiorelli introduced the practice of following the line of the roads, and of connecting different parts of the site.[53] This method was not necessarily the inspiration of Fiorelli himself: in the 1840s, instructions on how to excavate had also specified the need to dig systematically by town-block.[54] The crucial difference by the 1860s, however, was that the will to implement such a procedure was now present. This is partly the result of the changing aims of the excavators: Fiorelli's predecessors had been concerned primarily with retrieving treasures, whereas Fiorelli was interested in the development of the town as a whole.

In general, then, many of Fiorelli's reforms could be seen as the culmination of a gradual process, which had been evolving over the previous decade or so. Many of Fiorelli's reforms had been foreshadowed on a minor scale in the 1840s, and many were the fulfilment of proposals made by the 1848 commission. For example, Pompeii now finally received its own antiquarium, in the area of the 'Forum Baths'.[55] In general, his reforms appear to have been practical responses to problems encountered in administering the site and Museum, namely how to pursue excavation and document it, and how to arrange the collections in the Museum.[56]

In 1866, Fiorelli established a School of Archaeology at Pompeii, which lasted until 1875, when the establishment of a national Italian school of archaeology superseded it. The impetus for the School came from Fiorelli himself, who gained the support of King Victor Emmanuel II on a visit to Pompeii. It was not popular in other academic circles since Fiorelli had bypassed both the university and ministry structures in setting it up.[57] Nevertheless, this was actually quite appropriate, since his aim in establishing the School was not to create a training system that would parallel and rival that already provided by the University. Instead, he had perceived that one of the main problems faced by Pompeii was the lack of professionally trained workers who were skilled in practical aspects of archaeology, such as restoration and the description of finds. It is perhaps a reflection of this that only one of the students from this School, Eduardo Brizio, who was appointed to the chair of archaeology at Bologna in 1876, rose to the top of the academic ladder.[58] By contrast, three of the leading Pompeian scholars in the later nineteenth century, who became directors of the site or of Naples Museum – Michele Ruggiero, Giulio De Petra, and Antonio Sogliano – were all trained in the School.[59] Alongside this school, Fiorelli's revival of a journal for the excavations at Pompeii (*Giornale degli scavi di Pompei*) provided an outlet in which the students could publish their work.

One further innovation by Fiorelli was also to transform the whole character of Pompeii. It may sound paradoxical, but Fiorelli's introduction of an entrance fee for access to the site after 1860 dramatically opened it up to a wider cross-section of society. Both the Museum and the excavations now ceased to serve as a glorification of the royal court at Naples (now of course no longer there) by allowing only select visitors to view them. Instead, they became sources of public instruction and enlightenment, with an important role to play in educating the young about ancient Italian civilisation.[60] Again, this was not necessarily an abrupt change, but was the culmination of a gradual process over a couple of decades. Since the mid-1830s the new urban middle class at Naples had increasingly participated in activities that had previously been the preserve of aristocrats, such as attending the opera house, but it was only after 1860 that the widening cultural interests of this social group were catered for more fully.[61] As already outlined above, the same period had also brought a rapid increase in foreign visitors. Again, this trend became even more marked after 1860, not least since the first Italian tours of Thomas Cook were launched in 1864, which included an optional one-and-a-half day excursion to Naples, devoting a single day to visiting both Pompeii and Vesuvius, and half a day to exploring Naples itself.[62] Naturally, given that Herculaneum still lay underground, accessible only by tunnels, that site's era of mass tourism was yet to dawn. Cook even took over the funicular railway up the slopes of Vesuvius in 1888, in order to allow for briefer, more comfortable ascents of the volcano, but this was destroyed in the eruption of 1906.

Fiorelli's nomination as Senator in 1865 marked a further transitional point in his career, as his interests widened out beyond the Bay of Naples to the whole of Italy. This is reflected in his academic output, with the publication in 1867 of a work reporting archaeological finds in Italy from 1846 to 1866 (*Sulle scoperte archeologiche fatte in Italia dal 1846 al 1866*). This process culminated in 1875, when Fiorelli was promoted to a new post as Director General of Antiquities in Italy as a whole.[63] As a result, he was able to spread his local reforms from Pompeii to a country-wide stage, in particular introducing in 1876 the monthly archaeological reports known as *Notizie degli scavi di antichità*, an invaluable journal which is still published annually today. He sent a number of reports to the Ministry for Public Instruction suggesting ways of reorganising the pursuit of archaeology in Italy, and encouraged the reorganisation of museum collections, along with the publication of new catalogues. One example of his transferral of a technique from Pompeii to the wider stage of Italy can be seen from his proposal to divide Italy up into regions, based upon those devised by the emperor Augustus, as a framework for the administration of archaeological fieldwork.[64] This was in effect a more ambitious version of his division of Pompeii into regions a couple of decades earlier. Above all, he once again realised the importance of publishing inventories of museum holdings and excavation reports. It was not just a question of publishing pre-existing archives – he had to take an active role in gathering together relevant documents from the whole of Italy. Four volumes of previously unpublished documents relating to the history of museums in Italy appeared in 1878-80, containing about two thousand pages.[65] In many ways, then, the development of archaeology at Pompeii came to influence the publication and organisation of archaeology throughout Italy.

Despite a tendency both to hail Fiorelli as a hero of Unification and to run the risk of over-emphasising his real contribution to the study of Pompeii by misattributing to him some earlier innovations, it is hard to exaggerate his impact upon history of Pompeii. The honours granted to him in his lifetime – a marble bust in the Museum's coin room, a gold medallion issued in his honour by the Accademia dei Lincei, and a bronze bust in Pompeii's Forum – reflect his contemporaries' recognition of his contribution to local and national archaeology alike.[66] Whether he was primarily a political pragmatist, administrator, or archaeological innovator, Fiorelli arguably remains the individual who has had the greatest impact upon the way in which Pompeii has been both excavated and perceived.

6. Probing Beneath the Surface

The issue of great Jove, draw near, you Muses nine;
Help us to praise the blisfull plot of garden ground so fine.
The garden gives good food, and aid for leaches' cure;
The garden, full of great delight, his master doth allure.
Sweet salad herbs be here, and herbs of every kind,
The ruddy grapes, the seemly fruits be here at hand to find.
Here pleasure wanteth not, to make a man full fain;
Here marvellous the mixture is of solace, and of gain.

The Garden, Nicholas Grimald (?1519-?1562)

Fiorelli's legacy to Pompeian studies continued well into the twentieth century, as later scholars extended his technique of making plaster casts of human bodies to making casts of root cavities. Even by exploring only a few centimetres beneath the ground surface of AD 79, we can now construct a much richer picture of the ancient environment within the walls of Pompeii. On windy days, visitors to the site today might be forgiven for taking away the impression of a sterile town, dominated by swirling dust storms. It is hard to imagine that once the town was full of greenery, and that plants, shrubs, and trees flourished in both private gardens and public spaces. Admittedly, some areas of the town have been attractively land-scaped in relatively recent times, with, for example, the planting of a grove of evergreen oak trees in the 'Triangular Forum' some time before 1910 (an archive photograph reveals how bare this area looked before then).[1] This grove was planted by the archaeologist Giuseppe Spano, in order to realise his imaginative instinct that a sacred grove may once have flourished around the 'Doric Temple'. This is plausible enough, but is not based upon actual evidence that a grove once existed there. Other instances of modern planting, however, give a wholly misleading impression of the town's appearance, not least the grassing-over of a large expanse of the Forum's piazza, which was in fact originally paved with limestone slabs.[2] It requires a leap of the imagination to repopulate the town not only with its human inhabitants, but also with domestic and working animals such as dogs and

97

donkeys, and to hear the birdsong produced by both wild birds and birds reared in the town's aviaries or dovecotes.[3]

Today's visitor has only to observe the modern countryside around the ancient site to perceive something of the scale of this problem. In contrast to the rather arid-looking site, almost every square inch of the surrounding countryside is cultivated, with flowers and vegetables being grown even under the road bridges, and right up to the railway line. Several factors combine to make this region of Campania particularly fertile: the region's favourable climate, its mineral-rich soil (the result of volcanic activity) and its high water-table.[4] The Romans summed up its privileged relationship with nature in the phrase 'productive Campania' (*Campania felix*).[5]

An impression of the town's colourful environment emerges from paintings of gardens found in Pompeii. These depict verdant scenes with luxuriant foliage inhabited by birds with such a degree of realism that sometimes species are identifiable (see Plate XIII).[6] At the rear of the peristyle in the 'House of Marine Venus' (II.iii.3), a painted garden appears beyond the actual peristyle garden. The scene to its right depicts a basin, which has attracted a pigeon to its rim, and beneath it a heron. The basin is attractively represented among shrubs and flowers, which include a myrtle bush with white flowers, an oleander bush in blossom, a rose-bush in flower, and a tree with yellow apples.[7] As Pierre Grimal suggests, it may be that such paintings represent the sort of garden that someone wished to possess, but could not actually do so.[8] Such paintings do not always imitate real life exactly, for some scenes include fantastical details (see Plate XIV). In contrast to the realistic panel on the right in the 'House of Marine Venus', the central panel depicts a Botticelli-like scene of Venus floating upon a seashell, accompanied by two cupids, one riding on a dolphin.[9] Likewise, some paintings also lead the viewer's eye through a garden into the world beyond.[10] This world can be basically realistic, as in the 'House of the Amazons' (VI.ii.14) where a vista of the sea lies beyond the garden, or fantastical, as in the 'House of Orpheus' (VI.xiv.20), where a depiction of Orpheus charming the wild beasts in a mythological rural setting is framed by two realistic garden paintings.[11] However realistic such paintings may appear to be, therefore, they are not straightforward images of actual gardens: consequently, our image of Pompeian gardens might be rather distorted if we created it on the basis of this artistic evidence alone.

As our earlier chapters have shown, the earliest excavators at Pompeii were not at all interested in reconstructing the town's natural environment, and it was not until the late nineteenth/early twentieth centuries that excavators started to make occasional comments on evidence for plants. In 1910, for example, Spano found root cavities in four peristyle gardens, recording in one case that he had found the cavities left by the roots of various small trees, or perhaps of large plants, planted here and there in no particular arrangement.[12] Since he did not detail the size, shape, and exact location of these cavities, this information is of limited use. Shortly afterwards, Spinazzola first modified Fiorelli's method of making plaster casts of human bodies for making plaster casts of tree-root cavities, in the rear garden of the 'House of the Moralist' (III.iv.2-3), but these casts have been damaged over the years.[13] Some time later, Maiuri, in turn, made a number of casts of large tree-root cavities, which have survived intact. Visitors today can still see the casts he made of the cavities of the tall plane trees that provided shade in the Large Palaestra and in the open space around the Amphitheatre (see Plate XV).[14]

It was not, however, until the 1960s and 1970s that the American scholar Wilhelmina Jashemski first tried to identify systematically the location and character of all the gardens in Pompeii, supplementing her archaeological investigations with material drawn from the archives. As a result of her work, we can now reconstruct a town full of colour and life, with ornamental gardens and vegetable plots within houses, market gardens, and vineyards of various sizes. She too adopted the technique of making plaster casts of root cavities, but, unlike previous excavators, she used the technique on a wider range of cavities, not just large impressive tree roots. When trees and plants died in the aftermath of the eruption, their roots decayed, so that gradually the cavities left behind became filled by volcanic debris. When excavating a new area of the town, the debris, or lapilli, is removed for several metres until the ancient ground level is reached. At this point, lapilli-filled cavities become visible on the surface. These can be painstakingly cleared of lapilli, and then filled anew with cement. When this hardens, the soil from around the cast is removed, and often the shape of the root can be identified as a specific plant, such as a vine or plane tree (see Plate XVI).[15] In addition, Jashemski studied soil contours, which revealed the presence of planting beds and irrigation channels, and analysed floral and faunal remains, such as pollen and animal bones.

Jashemski's research has made it only too clear how much information about the town's environment has been irretrievably lost. As she herself

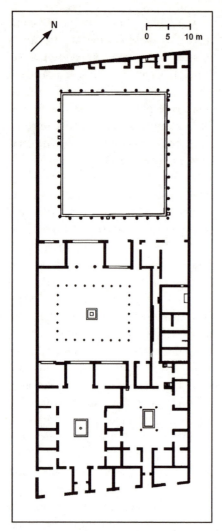

Fig. 9. Plan of the 'House of the Faun' (VI.xii.2).

lamented, 'few excavators have been interested in soil contours, root cavities, or plant remains, and a vast amount of precious evidence that could have been recovered only at the time of excavation has been lost forever'.[16] She was, however, able to recover a partial picture of the gardens in areas excavated during the 1950s, when the purpose of the excavations had been chiefly to procure large quantities of lapilli for use as hard-core in road construction. The speed and focus of these excavations meant that often a thin layer of lapilli was left covering the original ground surface. Where this surface had not been unduly damaged by the passage of trucks over it, Jashemski's team was able to remove the final covering of lapilli, revealing soil contours and lapilli-filled cavities. In addition, newly excavated areas produced striking evidence for cultivation.

It comes as no surprise to find that grand dwellings contained suitably impressive gardens. That much was already evident from excavations before Jashemski. The 'House of the Faun' (VI.xii.2), which occupies a whole insula, contains a large garden in the first peristyle, beyond the *atrium* where the famous statuette of the faun was displayed (Fig. 9). Nothing is known about the plants grown here because of its early date of excavation (1830-2) and because of bombardment during the Second World War. The elegance of the area is clearly indicated, however, by the presence of the striking Alexander the Great mosaic in the *exedra* on the north side of the garden, and of the marble fountain and pool in its centre.[17] Excavation of the pre-AD 79 levels in this house has revealed a changing use of space. In the second century BC, a kitchen garden occupied the area at the rear, which was later replaced by a peristyle (an open courtyard surrounded by a portico). This might seem to lend support to Grimal's hypothesis that kitchen gardens declined in popularity, being replaced by ornamental gardens that were more integrated into the overall architectural form of the house: visitors could now enjoy a view extending from the main entrance right through to the rear peristyle garden.[18] We shall see later, however, that this hypothesis is by no means true everywhere in Pompeii, although it may perhaps be accurate of the very grandest residences, of which the 'House of the Faun' is undoubtedly one.

A partial impression can be gained of ornamental gardens by visiting the 'House of the Vettii' (VI.xv.1) (Fig. 10, and see Plate XVII). The substantial peristyle garden at the rear of this house has been replanted with shrubs, and many pieces of sculpture are on display there. The current planting pattern and choice of vegetation is based only upon guesswork, since the house's excavators in 1894-5 observed only that traces of planting beds were still visible, without publishing accurate plans of these, and without taking note of any root cavities. Originally, too, the whole garden would have been full of the sound of water – twelve fountain statuettes directed their jets of water into eight marble basins standing around its edge. The lead pipes supplying them were found in good condition.[19] Whereas the water features were observed at the time of excavation because they included fountains, statuettes and lead piping, the accompanying planting beds provoked little interest.

Of course, the excavators of the town's grand houses targeted them

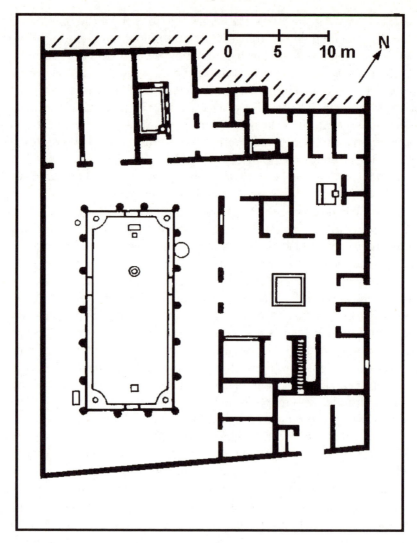

Fig. 10. Plan of the 'House of the Vettii' (VI.xv.1).

because of their fine paintings and sculpture. Jashemski sought instead to recover their gardens, and in several cases where it was no longer possible to recover primary archaeological evidence, her work from archival records highlighted the rather surprising fact that grand houses might also contain large produce gardens (something which requires us to qualify Grimal's model of the decline of kitchen gardens, mentioned above). For example, about a third of the 'House of Pansa' (VI.vi.1), which occupied an entire insula, was taken up by gardens – a peristyle garden with an ornamental pool, and a rear garden for produce, with rectangular plots separated by paths and irrigation channels.[20] In fact, Spano had already suggested in 1910 that the 'House of the Silver Wedding' (V.ii.1) contained a large irrigated vegetable garden.[21]

Such produce gardens were not always divided off from the elegance of the rest of the house. In the 'House of the Ephebe' (I.vii.11), an elaborate outdoor dining-couch, or *triclinium*, was located next to a vegetable garden.[22] In fact, as Nicholas Purcell has suggested was the case in luxury villas, impressive Pompeian houses may have commonly juxtaposed the ornamental and the functional (or, as he puts it, *elegantia* and *utilitas*).[23] It may not even have always been clear whether a particular feature was intended to be primarily decorative or useful. The centre of the peristyle garden of the 'Estate of Julia Felix' (II.iv) was attractively dominated by a series of four connecting fishponds with marble bridges (Fig. 11, and see Plate XVIII). Likewise, a pool in which fish scales and backbones were found formed the focal point of the garden in the 'House of the Centenary' (IX.viii.6).[24] Such pools were not just ornamental attractions, as is the case with the koi carp that swim about in garden ponds today, but provided food. At the same time, the presence of mosaics depicting fish elsewhere, in other water-features, shows that the idea of decorativeness was not altogether absent.[25]

In addition to containing cultivated land, these large houses appear to have acted as bases from which land outside the town could be managed. The most convincing evidence for this was the discovery of a large number of agricultural tools (including fifteen vine-pruning knives, seven hoes, a shovel, rake, and scythe), together with a small wagon, in the 'House of the Menander' (I.x.4) (see Plate XIX). Only a small portion of the house in question appears to have been cultivated, with, for example, a small secluded kitchen garden. If occupants of this house were indeed using these tools, it seems plausible that they were taking them outside the town to cultivate land belonging to the same household around Pompeii. At the same time, however, caution is necessary, since the source of this theory was Maiuri's keenness to identify the skeleton found there as that of the household's domestic and farm manager.[26]

Alongside these rather grand properties, even relatively modest houses and workplaces contained garden areas. Plants were squeezed into even the smallest spaces in houses, in order to make some contact with nature.[27]

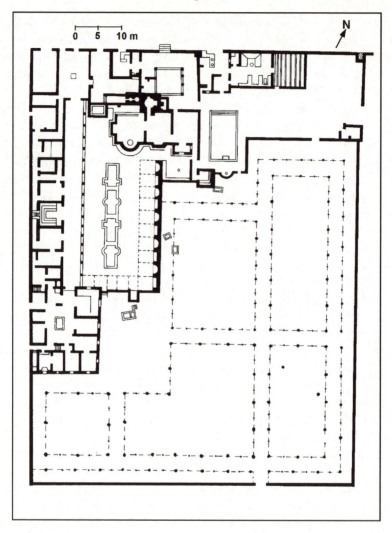

Fig. 11. Plan of the 'Estate of Julia Felix' (II.iv).

In one small house, I.ii.15, there was no space available for a garden, but around the *impluvium* ran a low masonry wall, the top of which was filled with soil where plants might grow in the absence of a proper garden. Elsewhere, in the 'House of M. Fabius Amandio' (I.vii.2-3), a small raised garden, complete with a tiny pool fed by rainwater from the roof, was squeezed into the house, in a light well at the rear of the *atrium*. In order to compensate for the rather cramped conditions, an impression was created that the garden extended further than it really did by means of a garden painting on the wall behind.[28] In slightly larger, though still relatively modest, houses, dining 'al fresco' could be catered for, with the provision of an outdoor *triclinium* shaded by a vine-covered pergola. House I.xiv.2 has preserved evidence for the flexible, multi-purpose nature of such gardens. Here the shaded *triclinium* stands in a garden where Jashemski found four large trees at its edges (including an ancient olive tree and a fig tree), five irregular rows of smaller trees, planting pots alongside the north wall for grafting trees, and carbonised beans grown between the trees.[29] Small gardens might also enhance the ambience of a workplace. A converted house identified as a shop where fish-sauce (*garum*) was sold, I.xii.8, contained storerooms in its rear courtyard, with the peristyle acting as a work area. Even though it was a fairly small space, the peristyle housed two large fig trees. An illusion of spaciousness was created once again by the addition of a large garden painting along the rear wall of the peristyle.[30] This technique of creating a sense of space by the judicious placement of a 'trompe-l'oeil' garden painting is found elsewhere too.[31] In VII.vi.7, plants grew in beds along the peristyle's portico, behind which a garden painting on the rear wall gave the impression of the garden extending further, or even of the existence of another garden altogether.[32] Most striking, perhaps, was the painting in the 'House of the Amazons' (VI.ii.14), now destroyed, but preserved in a modern water-colour painting, where the eye was artificially led from a fence into a garden, and beyond to the sea.[33]

One of the most notable achievements of Jashemski's project was the revelation that the large area known as the cattle market was in fact a large commercial vineyard. The *insula* directly to the north of the Amphitheatre (II.v) was first excavated in 1755, and later again in 1814. The area was variously identified as a cattle market, or as a burial or banqueting place for gladiators, or as the place where animals were kept penned up for hunting exhibitions in the Amphitheatre. It seems that these identifications were suggested on the basis of its location, the discovery of bones of various animals, and the presence of a masonry *triclinium* near its entrance from the Amphitheatre. Further investigation during the 1950s revealed two rooms equipped for winemaking. Jashemski started to re-assess the *insula* in 1966. By 1968, 1,423 vine-root cavities had been identified, increasing to 2,014 by 1970.[34] It has now been replanted with vines, recreating an impression of its original appearance (Fig. 12, and see Plate XX). On one side of the vineyard was a small building where wine

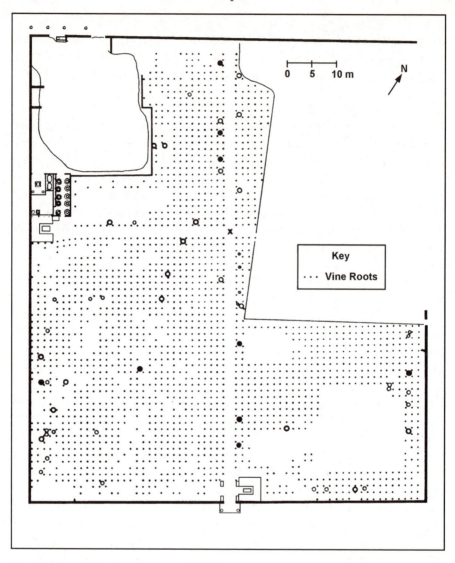

Fig. 12. Plan of the large vineyard (II.v).

was made, enclosing a pressroom and an open shed with ten embedded storage jars, or *dolia*, where the grape juice could be stored for fermentation. Each *dolium* had a capacity of about 275 gallons, which would fill about forty *amphorae*.[35] This vineyard is unusually large, and its possession of a winepress distinguishes it from smaller establishments, where the grapes were crushed by foot. Grimal interpreted the vineyard as primarily de-signed for pleasure, a venue for feasts and banquets. He labelled it 'a piece of countryside that is thus included in a garden designed for pleasure'.[36] Certainly some people wined and dined here: two *triclinia* are located in the vineyard, and Jashemski found eleven bones with cleaver marks, where they had been split to obtain marrow, indicating that they represent debris from meals. The primary purpose of the vineyard, though, was the production of wine rather than the provision of a banqueting venue. This wine was probably sold from the shop abutting onto the 'Street of Abundance'.[37]

Nor was this the only example of commercial agriculture within the town's walls. Several other smaller vineyards, orchards, and market gar-dens also came into view through Jashemski's excavations. These are not quite on the same scale as the large vineyard, but are not negligible in size: one orchard (I.xxii) appears to have contained about three hundred trees.[38] Such premises would presumably have produced goods for the local urban market. Vines grown in the 'Inn of Euxinus' (I.xi.10-11), near the Amphi-theatre, would have supplied customers with home-produced wine (Fig. 13). This inn has a counter at its main entrance, where customers could be served refreshments. In addition, a large open area, also accessible from the street, could accommodate customers who wished to take their time. Thirty-two vines planted in irregular rows produced grapes which could be fermented on the premises in two large *dolia*, found partially embedded in the ground, each with a capacity of about 100 gallons. Jashemski calculated that a vineyard of this size might have produced up to about 75 gallons per annum, so we might appear to have a discrepancy between the capacity of the *dolia* (200 gallons) and the productive capacity of the vineyard (75 gallons). But this was not the only cultivated plot, since in addition, a large open area at the rear of the connecting house was also planted with vines. The innkeeper did not limit himself to selling home-produced wine, however: some wine *amphorae* were found labelled with the painted inscription giving the address to which they were to be delivered – 'at Pompeii / near the Amphitheatre / to the innkeeper Euxinus' (*Pompeis / ad amphitheatr / Euxino coponi*).[39] A similar degree of self-sufficiency is found in the 'Inn of the Gladiators' (I.xx.1), where grapes were grown and wine made on the premises.[40] The discovery of three olive presses, a number of winepresses, and a threshing floor within the town indicates that it was not uncommon for produce to be processed as well as grown within the town.[41]

An important characteristic of production in Pompeii was the predomi-

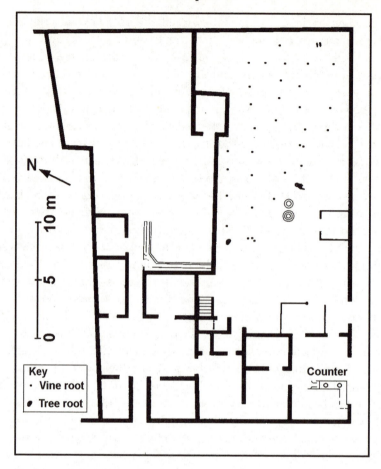

Fig. 13. Plan of the 'Inn of Euxinus' (I.xi.10-11).

nance of polyculture, the simultaneous cultivation of different crops together, with vines, olives, and vegetables being grown side by side. For
example, beans may have been grown in between rows of fruit trees in the
garden of a small house on the 'Nucerian Street' (I.xiv.2), where carbonised
beans and five rows of tree-root cavities were discovered.[42] Similarly, the
market-garden of the 'House of the Ship Europa' (I.xv.3) included fruit
trees, vines, and vegetable plots, as well as perhaps a source of potters'
clay.[43] Given that the plaster-cast technique is only of use for recovering
relatively large cavities, such as vine roots and stakes, because lapilli were
too large to fall down into small root cavities, vegetables and flowers are
under-represented in the surviving archaeological sample. Nevertheless,

the presence of irrigation channels is suggestive of other crops since vines do not require much water.

In addition to the production of edible foodstuffs, flowers were grown in some gardens, perhaps for making garlands and perfume, and non-edible plants and seedlings. The cavities in the 'Garden of the Fugitives' (I.xxi.2) may represent rose-bushes, since irrigation channels and many fragments of terracotta perfume containers were also found there. Likewise, fragments of glass perfume bottles and of terracotta unguent containers in the 'Garden of Hercules' (II.viii.6) suggest that it too was devoted to raising flowers.[44]

We still have only a partial picture of the gardens of Pompeii, therefore, since the archaeological evidence available is biased towards the recovery of trees and shrubs. Future research is possible, though, since although Jashemski's research was limited by the earlier destruction of evidence, a significant portion of the site remains to be excavated, and it is probable that this northeastern region also contains horticultural areas.

Furthermore, we still have only tantalising glimpses of the environment beyond the walls of Pompeii. Careful examination of newly excavated areas can provide a detailed snapshot of mixed agricultural production in a countryside estate, or *villa rustica*. The 'Villa Regina' at Boscoreale, a few kilometres to the north of Pompeii, for example, was excavated only during the late 1970s and early 1980s. The identification of 300 vine cavities revealed that part of the area immediately surrounding the *villa* was planted as a vineyard, but thirty-four tree-root cavities, together with carbonised olives and almonds, illustrated that once again mixed cultivation was the norm outside, as well as inside, the walls of Pompeii. Not all cultivation was designed primarily for profit, however: the planting of vines around the sanctuary of Dionysus just to the south of Pompeii was designed not only as a suitable homage to the god of wine, but also as a way of creating a pleasant, shady ambience in which to hold banquets in his honour.[45]

Despite these limitations, our picture of land use within the town has been dramatically transformed by Jashemski's research, and its significance does not stop there. Instead, the pattern of land use at Pompeii is relevant to our interpretation of other pre-industrial towns, their relationship with surrounding areas of countryside, and their economic activities. In his standard work on Roman gardens, Grimal warns against attributing too much significance to the evidence at Pompeii and Herculaneum, on the grounds that their fortuitous archaeological survival masks their relative insignificance in antiquity, and risks allowing them to acquire an importance out of all proportion to their original significance.[46] This warning is well made, of course, but nevertheless we might actually consider this fact from the opposite point of view, namely that the very insignificance of Pompeii makes it a valuable historical tool in assessing the character of an ordinary ancient Italian town. In this way, Pompeii might be regarded as providing a desirable alternative perspective in a historical record that is otherwise largely dominated by the city of Rome itself.

Ancient towns have often been interpreted as essentially non-productive spaces, reliant upon the countryside to provide them with foodstuffs.[47] The city of Rome is rightly regarded as the paradigm for this model, which has informed the view of Roman towns among historians of later periods. A typical statement of this view can be found at the start of a recent discussion of the development of medieval towns, where Roman towns are considered to have been 'more consumers than producers of goods and services'.[48] Jashemski's revelation of Pompeii as a town of agricultural production has required a re-assessment of this view. Various responses have been made to her picture. First, the scale of production within Pompeii has been dismissed as insignificant: 'We shall ignore the recent discoveries by W. Jashemski of vegetable gardens and vineyards within the city walls. They are an important reminder that we should not conceive of town and country as completely separate spheres – if such reminder were necessary. But they are too small to affect estimates of aggregate supply.'[49] Secondly, a line of special pleading has been adopted in order to explain the presence of the large vineyard to the north of the Amphitheatre. The decision to devote prime land here and elsewhere in the town to cultivation is seen as 'a purely voluntaristic choice on behalf of a community not nearly so concerned with competition and materialism as was previously supposed'.[50] The suggestion that the people of Pompeii were not particularly concerned with profit conflicts with the general atmosphere of the town. Visitors to one house (VII.i.46), for example, were greeted with the words 'Hail profit!' in the paving of the entranceway, and elsewhere the leading producer of *garum* advertised his business with mosaics in his *atrium*.[51] It also ignores the commercial aspect of growing wine and food for profit.

Rather than dismissing the evidence altogether or explaining it away in non-economic terms, our picture of cultivation within the walls of Pompeii can most meaningfully be assessed against the background of recent research on medieval urbanisation. In 1979, the same year as Jashemski published the first volume on the gardens of Pompeii, Catherine Delano Smith explored what she termed the 'urbanized countryside and country-fied town' in western Mediterranean Europe during the medieval period.[52] A more recent study of the Mediterranean world has supported this picture, insisting that agricultural land commonly existed within towns: 'There were large open spaces – uncultivated, agricultural land, or orchards – in even the largest and apparently most crowded of Mediterranean cities: Pompeii, Rome, Barcelona, Milan, Cairo.'[53] This is not to argue that towns were autarchic, independently producing all their own necessary food, but neither does it seem plausible any longer to regard towns as simply parasitic upon the countryside. Nor is it convincing to suggest that Pompeii only included horticultural spaces because the town was in a state of economic crisis during its last period.[54] We do not need to invoke the alleged abandonment of the town following 'the earthquake' of AD 62 to explain why some land within the town was under cultivation. Early medieval towns in Italy also included agricultural land inside their walls, something that no longer has to be explained as a new phenomenon of the medieval period, representing the 'ruralisation' of cities. Rather, it suggests a striking degree of continuity between ancient and medieval towns in Italy.[55]

Although, therefore, the inclusion of agricultural land within the walls of Pompeii might now seem unexceptional in terms of the use of land in pre-industrial towns in general, the fact remains that the reasons under-lying such land use may differ according to the particular historical situation. For example, Delano Smith suggests that a major motivation for cultivating land within medieval towns may have been to safeguard food supply for the town's inhabitants in time of siege.[56] This also seems to explain the inclusion of undeveloped areas, largely gardens and fields, within the defensive circuit of Milan still later, during the sixteenth century.[57] The inhabitants of Pompeii, however, would not have been worried about being besieged by hostile forces during the late first century BC and throughout the first century AD, since peace had been guaranteed since the time of the conquest and unification of the Italian peninsula by Rome in the early first century BC. At the same time, it is possible to suggest geographical reasons why we should not unthinkingly take Pompeii as our model town for other towns the length and breadth of Italy. As has already been noted earlier, the town was founded upon unusually fertile soil, allowing the adoption of an intensive system of polyculture. Furthermore, much of the cultivated land within Pompeii is situated on south-facing slopes, a factor which may have compensated for choosing to set aside such areas within the town for cultivation by enabling even higher levels of production than elsewhere.[58] Finally, little is known about Pompeii's relationship with its hinterland and its role as a river harbour, both of which may have affected land use within the town itself. So, many new questions about the environmental character of Pompeii and the relationship of this urban centre with its surrounding countryside can now be raised as a result of penetrating beneath the ground surface of AD 79. By digging still deeper, however, we can now extend the scope of such questioning much further back in time, even uncovering some green spaces in pre-Roman Pompeii.

7. Probing Ever Deeper

Herculaneum and Pompeii next to it, past which the River Sarno flows, were held by the Oscans. Then came the Etruscans and the Pelasgians, and after that the Samnites. These too were thrown out of these places.

Strabo, *Geography* 5.4.8

For well over a hundred years, the excavators of Pompeii were content to reveal only the latest layer of life in the town, as preserved by the eruption. Their aim was to clear away the volcanic material deposited in the eruption in order to uncover the town in its destroyed state and to retrieve its victims' treasures. They showed little interest in the earlier history of the town, despite the fact that the discovery of inscriptions in Oscan, an Italic dialect, and allusions in ancient literature, such as the passage of Strabo's *Geography* cited above, provided clear reminders that the town had already experienced a long history before it was destroyed, and that it had only become Roman during its last 150 years or so, after Sulla had imposed a colony of his veterans upon the town in around 80 BC. Against the background of the nascent Risorgimento and the emerging interest in the ancient peoples of Italy, Fiorelli was one of the first to articulate a view of the town's early development by examining the layout of the town's roads and *insulae*, and by studying the Oscan inscriptions and literary accounts of Pompeii's origins. His enthusiasm for promoting awareness of the local histories of Italian towns also found expression in his establishment of a museum relating to the local history of Naples and in his participation in a commission for the preservation of monuments there.[1]

In the latter part of the nineteenth century, then, and especially by the early twentieth century, scholars became increasingly keen to recover the town's pre-Roman history. On the whole, though, instead of digging beneath the ground surface of AD 79, they sought to elucidate the earlier periods from structures surviving above ground level. This resulted in the somewhat paradoxical situation that, although Pompeii did play a key role in the development of archaeology as a discipline, the town itself remained a single-layer site. Until the 1930s/40s, when Maiuri embarked upon a series of stratigraphic soundings at various points on the site, the town's pre-Roman history was reconstructed mainly from evidence visible above the ground surface of AD 79. One of the most influential techniques depended upon the assumption that the various masonry styles visible in the town's standing structures directly reflected the relative antiquity of their walls.[2] For example, it became generally accepted that structures made up of Sarno limestone had survived since the sixth/fifth century BC, whereas the use of Nucerian tufa was taken to indicate a second-century BC date of construction.[3] Variations on this theme have been composed over the years, with a more recent commentator suggesting that the oldest limestone houses should be associated with a Samnite invasion in the late fourth/third century BC (rather than the sixth/fifth century).[4]

Furthermore, the principle was established that such changes in construction technique were the direct reflection of changes in the composition of the town's inhabitants. In particular, the succession of different peoples – Oscans, Etruscans, Pelasgians, and Samnites – 'known' from the passage of Strabo cited above to have occupied the town in turn was thought to have brought about the adoption of different building techniques.[5] Writing from the perspective of the late first century BC/early first century AD, Strabo considered the development of Pompeii to be typical of a significant number of towns, which he characterised as experiencing a sequence of refoundations by successive occupants. His view was that each time new occupants took over such a town, it took on a new identity, and he set these refoundations against the general historical context of ancient migrations of peoples.[6] Although Strabo's Oscans, Etruscans, and Samnites might seem to emerge from the archaeological evidence, the Pelasgians are generally ignored in modern accounts of Pompeii's history. The basic assumption that the waves of invading peoples brought with them into Pompeii a succession of construction techniques, and that these remained visible for centuries until the town was overwhelmed, has remained remarkably influential in studies of the town's history, but we might wish to challenge the assumption that cultural change was always the direct result of an invasion and migration of a new people into the town. Changes in what might be termed an 'archaeological culture' do not necessarily reflect the input of a particular ethnic group.[7] Instead, it is more likely that what we are looking at is a complex cultural system derived from a mixture of influences, and it is often a thankless task to try to separate out different cultural trends and associate them with a particular group of inhabitants.

114

Only recently has the antiquity of houses built using large square-cut, or ashlar, blocks of Sarno limestone been tested against stratigraphic soundings carried out at the foundations of their façades. Analysis of the pottery evidence recovered from such soundings now suggests that these houses were built much later than previously supposed, probably towards the end of the third century BC.[8] Nor is this an isolated example of the potential of standing structures to generate a false picture of Pompeii's pre-Roman phases. The attractive suggestion that the construction of the portico in the 'Triangular Forum' was part of a major reorganisation of the sacred precinct there to include a running-track in the second century BC, indicative of the wider hellenisation of the town as a whole, has been thrown into doubt by recent stratigraphic investigations suggesting that the portico dates only from the Augustan period.[9] Clearly, building techniques alone cannot be relied upon to give an accurate date for a structure, but neither should we jettison this approach altogether since there does seem to have been a general trend moving from the use of local lava to Sarno limestone to Nucerian tufa, although it may be necessary to assign later dates to these phases.[10]

Alongside this idea of successive phases in the history of Pompeii, one of the main debates that arose, partly from Strabo's inclusion of the Etruscans in his list of dominant peoples, was whether or not Pompeii became an Etruscan town. In assessing this question mainly on the basis of literary evidence, because of the lack of relevant archaeological exploration, discussions in the 1930s debated whether or not the Etruscans had played a crucial role in developing Pompeii into a proper town.[11] Whereas Roger Carrington attributed a vital role in the urbanisation of Pompeii to the Etruscans, Axel Boëthius argued that the Etruscans had probably dominated only a small core of the town in Regions VII and VIII for a short period in the early fifth century BC. In the absence of hard evidence, both scholars had to appeal to probability in constructing their arguments. In particular, in interpreting the visible structures of the town's defensive circuit, Boëthius considered it improbable that such a large area had been enclosed by walls as early as 500 BC. He suggested instead that the town was enlarged and its impressive defences built only in the wake of a Samnite immigration at the end of the fifth century BC.[12]

Shortly afterwards, Maiuri undertook to explore by excavation the antiquity of the town's walls, but even his extensive analysis of the dating of the defences drew more upon the existing historical framework than upon archaeological data. Indeed, despite the fact that he observed the presence of the first phase of the wall constructed out of blocks of dark-grey 'pappamonte' tufa, he omitted this phase altogether from his analysis of the walls' development because it did not fit into his historical frame-work.[13] It is only as a result of recent stratigraphic soundings at various points in the walls that a surprisingly early date for this earliest 'pappamonte' phase has been established, namely the first half of the sixth century BC.[14] As a result of studying the new data from soundings rather than seeking to insert the fortifications into a political and historical framework connected with hypothetical warfare and invasions, the second phase of the walls, a double curtain of limestone, now appears likely to date from the fifth century BC, and the third phase combining limestone and tufa blocks may have been built towards the end of the fourth or early third century BC.[15]

This basic picture will doubtless be refined in future years as more soundings are carried out, which may well reveal minor alterations to the walls within these phases. Indeed some intimation of possible future results has already emerged. In Chiaramonte Treré's 'sounding 3', in the area between the 'Nolan Gate' and Tower VIII, an intermediate phase in the limestone wall has been revealed, where a short stretch has been rebuilt in small limestone blocks, the result perhaps of structural collapse or enemy attack.[16] Similarly, there is a section of wall to the east of the 'Nucerian Gate' where 'lava tenera' (another volcanic stone, similar in appearance to 'pappamonte' tufa) is used rather than 'pappamonte'. Until this is excavated it remains unclear whether the two materials were used together at the same time, or whether the lava wall partly replaced the one in 'pappamonte' at some date.[17] The overall pattern of development in the town's defences now needs to be related to the gradual urbanisation of the town within the walls, working from archaeological data, rather than to a superimposed historical framework taken from ancient authors.

In addition to the problem of how to assess the possibility that Etrus-cans were present in Pompeii without digging down to the relevant layers, a second major problem lay in the necessity of distinguishing between Greek and Etruscan influence.[18] The Greek colonies of Pithekoussai and Cumae appear to have extended their spheres of influence in Campania as a whole during the seventh century BC, with the result that native cultures in the Sarno Valley adopted some hellenised characteristics in this period, while links between Campania and Etruria can be discerned already in the Early Iron Age. The cultural exchange between Greeks in Campania and Etruscans was conducted in both directions, with the borrowing of Greek words and names in the Etruscan language and, in particular from the sixth century, a wide range of Etruscan material goods appearing in Campania. The extent of cultural interchange between these two peoples makes it difficult to categorise with certainty any particular artefact as being either more 'Greek' or more 'Etruscan' in the absence of accompanying linguistic evidence.[19] This distinction is especially unclear at Pompeii because of 'the mixture of Greek, native and Etruscan'.[20] One of the oldest structures at Pompeii in the 'Triangular Forum', commonly known as the 'Doric Temple', has been assessed by two different scholars as being both purely Greek and not particularly Greek.[21] Similarly, the god of the other early sanctuary, Apollo, has now been claimed as being as much an Etruscan as a Greek deity in this period, and the architectural terracottas found re-used in the sanctuary's 'hellenistic' phase have been regarded as Etruscan in character.[22] A sense almost of desperation creeps into Carrington's remark in assessing Pompeii's early defensive wall as more Italic in character than Greek: 'The idea, then, of direct Greek influence in the building of those early walls must be abandoned. They seem, rather, to be Italic walls trying, as it were, to "look" Greek'.[23]

Increasingly, however, in recent times, the discovery of pottery bearing Etruscan graffiti in the 'House of the Faun' (VI.xii.2), the 'House of Ganymede' (VII.xiii.4, 17), I.ix.11, and above all the Temple of Apollo, provides clear evidence for some sort of contact with Etruscans at Pompeii.[24] Although little significance can reliably be attributed to the few pottery fragments from the other contexts, the sixth-century deposits from the Temple of Apollo, which contained twenty inscribed 'bucchero' pottery fragments, together with Corinthian, Laconian, and Attic pots, and architectural terracottas, are potentially more enlightening.[25] Admittedly, such graffiti does not unequivocally point to Etruscans living in Pompeii; but, despite the presence of many fragments of Greek pottery, no graffito in Greek has been found, suggesting that the Etruscan graffiti may reflect local writing habits. Furthermore, the chronological distribution of material in the temple, with the Etruscan graffiti in the first quarter of the sixth century marking the start of a period of abundant material down until about 475 BC, when it suddenly ceases, is suggestive of some sort of wider social, economic, or political shift within Pompeii as a whole. The date at which Etruscans may have had a significant impact upon Pompeii still remains open for discussion, though: two fragments of locally produced pottery bearing Etruscan graffiti, which seem to date from the fourth century BC, have also been found in a necropolis at Pompeii. This might

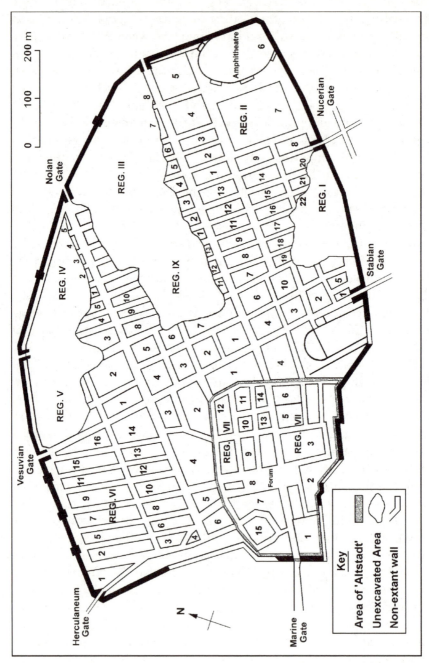

Fig. 14. Pompeii, with the 'Altstadt' highlighted.

imply that Etruscan influence lasted for up to three hundred years, rather longer than has hitherto been supposed.[26] Nevertheless, the resemblance of the Etruscan lettering on this local pottery to that on contemporary Oscan inscriptions suggests that we are not dealing with a straightforward model of cultural influence, in which the Etruscans were dominant over other local cultural elements.

Now that it seems likely that Etruscans may well have been present at Pompeii, more research is needed to test the hypothesis that Pompeii may have been some sort of Etruscan foundation resulting from the synoecism of villages along the Sarno Valley.[27] It is not impossible that the coincidence of Pompeii's urban development at an important harbour location and the abrupt decline of nearby villages in the valley, such as San Marzano and San Valentino, may reflect the Etruscans' desire to expand their influence in Campania.

The most important result of this recent research on the town's walls is that it has confirmed what had seemed intrinsically unlikely, namely that the whole modern site covering sixty-six hectares was already enclosed within this defensive circuit by the sixth century BC. This may partly be explained by the decision to follow the most defensive line in the natural landscape in building the walls, and also by the likelihood that, as in AD 79, land use within the town walls was not exclusively urban in character, but included cultivated areas.[28] Nevertheless, the revelation that the whole of the extensive area was fortified at such an early date raises the issue of the relationship of what is generally known as the 'Altstadt' and the area which lies beyond it but within the walls. An 'Altstadt', the original nucleus of the settlement covering an area of about fourteen hectares, appears to be revealed by the irregular layout of streets in the area around the Temple of Apollo and the Forum (Fig. 14).[29] In the past, only two alternative models for Pompeii's early development had been suggested: either the whole town was established in a single, unified phase, or the 'Altstadt' was occupied first, with the rest of the town developing outwards from it.[30] Although a hypothetical model for the town's gradual expansion within the walls, based upon the evidence of the patterns formed by the orientation of groups of *insulae*, still seems to make sense, such a hypothesis needs to take account of contradictions and complexities in stratigraphic evidence.[31]

Exploration in the 'House of the Terracotta Shapes' (VII.iv.62), which, on the 'Altstadt' hypothesis, should be immediately beyond this early core of settlement, did indeed support the idea that this area remained unde-

119

veloped in the archaic period. The earliest datable pottery finds in the area
to the east of what became the *tablinum* suggest that structures were first
constructed here towards the end of the fourth or early third century BC.
It seems that a private house was constructed here only during the second
century BC. Underneath this lies a series of rooms, whose paving pattern
implies the existence here of couches, probably surrounded by a portico.
This complex presents us with an unexpected glimpse of social and cultural practices in third-century BC Pompeii, since it is best interpreted as
a public banqueting hall, possibly influenced by Greek customs. It is,
however, impossible to reconstruct with any degree of certainty the character of the activities which took place here purely on the basis of
archaeology: it is also quite likely that the Samnite Pompeians may have
been following non-Greek local cultural practices, since a similar structure
has been identified elsewhere in Campania, at Buccino, where Greek
influences seem unlikely.[32] The chronology of these developments here
suggests that the *insulae* in this area around the 'Nucerian Street', along
with the 'Street of Fortune' and 'Street of Nola' may only have been
established during the third century BC. Nevertheless, the excavators
admitted that, despite the fact that their investigations had failed to find
archaic material, except perhaps in one small pit in the area of the later
atrium, sixth-century material had informally come to light in the *insula*
during the construction in the modern era of a new guardhouse and the
installation of electricity. Such random finds are not sufficient to undermine the conclusions of the digging conducted under controlled
circumstances, but they do at least raise a question mark about whether
or not archaic activity really was occurring just beyond the 'Altstadt'.[33]

On the other hand, positive evidence that not all of the area within the
town walls was fully inhabited and built up in the sixth century BC has
emerged from excavations in VI.v. In six different samples of layers dating
from the seventh and sixth centuries BC, significant quantities of carbonised wood (123 fragments) were found. These fragments were unusually
large for this sort of find (0.5-5 cm) and were identified as being predomi-
nantly of beech (119 fragments), with only a single fragment of pine and
three of holm oak. That these fragments might have been offcuts from
carpentry or remnants from ovens or hearths has been excluded by the
high rate of fungus present, which suggests rather that they came from
dead branches which had fallen to the ground and which had then been
rotting naturally. It therefore seems highly likely that there was an area
of beech wood within the walls of Pompeii during the archaic period,

although it cannot be determined whether it was naturally occurring or deliberately planted.[34]

Further evidence has emerged from I.ix.11-12, suggesting that activities within the walls of archaic Pompeii were not necessarily urban in character. Plant remains found in the pre-Roman layers suggest that grain was de-husked and cleaned here, probably prior to hand-milling. The waste products of such a process were discovered in a number of layers, but virtually disappear from Roman phases, suggesting 'that grain was no longer being processed on the site as it became more fully urban in character'.[35] It certainly seems that our modern conception of the strict division between town and countryside is no more suitable for archaic Pompeii than for the town in AD 79, as we saw in Chapter 6.

Although, therefore, it now seems likely that the 'Altstadt' may still have been the area where settlement was most concentrated within the town's walls during the archaic period, albeit without its own fortifications, future discoveries may indicate the nature of land use in the areas beyond the 'Altstadt' within the walls. Because of the prevailing influence of the 'Altstadt' hypothesis, until recently most investigations looking for evidence of archaic Pompeii have tended to choose to dig within the 'Altstadt' area. The subsequent discovery of archaic material in such digs has then appeared to confirm the hypothesis that this was where early activity took place.[36] The occasional discovery of fragmentary archaic antefixes elsewhere, beyond the 'Altstadt', such as beneath the 'House of the Etruscan Column' (VI.xiv.20) and the 'House of Ganymede' (VII.xiii.4, 17) has been interpreted as evidence for isolated shrines in a semi-rural setting within the town's walls.[37] A rather different model is suggested, however, by Maiuri's discovery of 'pappamonte' structures together with fragments of 'bucchero' pottery on either side of the 'Street of Mercury' and along the first stretch of the 'Street of Abundance'.[38] This would seem to indicate the remains of housing rather than of sacred buildings, and implies that the two axial roads through the settlement, in addition to the area of the 'Altstadt', were occupied by houses.

A still more radical modification of our traditional picture of archaic Pompeii arises from recent investigations in the late 1990s in the southeast of the town, in I.ix, an area which, on the hitherto accepted model of the town's development, should have been one of the last areas within the walls to have been extensively developed in the third century BC.[39] Structures which have been interpreted as possibly representing foundation trenches for timber-framed or mud-brick construction, found in the deepest layers of I.ix.12 and dating from the sixth/fifth century BC, adhere to the same alignment as the later house structures built above them. This implies that the road system was already in existence here by the sixth century and that it influenced the settlement pattern.[40] Archaic pottery fragments have also been found beneath houses 10 and 3 in the same *insula*.[41] Whether or not the evidence gathered so far really does add up to 'a very much more substantial and organised development of the eastern half in the archaic period' now needs to be tested by further work, but we certainly have a much more complex picture of Pompeii's early development than we did even a decade ago.[42]

Whereas the dating of settlement beyond the 'Altstadt' has been put significantly earlier in this way, our dating of the standing structures still visible above the surface today has been set radically later than previously supposed. The use of Sarno limestone and *opus Africanum* in I.ix.12 would traditionally have been identified as 'archaic' characteristics, but the recent stratigraphic work there has revealed that the house was in fact only built in the first century BC.[43] Similarly, the visible remains of the supposedly 'archaic' 'House of the Etruscan Column' (VI.xiv.20) now appear to originate only in the second century BC.[44] The relevance of these isolated instances to other parts of the town has been tested more widely by a series of stratigraphic soundings carried out at the foundations of the façades of houses built in ashlar Sarno limestone. Analysis of the pottery sherds found there now suggests that the town developed rapidly only at the end of the third, rather than during the mid-fourth, century BC.[45] Before that, walls of beaten earth compressed within a wooden frame, such as have been recently identified beneath the third-century phase of the 'House of the Vestals' (VI.i.7, 25), and which may well have been missed by earlier excavators in the few cases where stratigraphic soundings were conducted, probably accounted for the town's earlier development.[46]

This hypothesis of a boom in private construction towards the end of the third century BC now seems to cohere nicely with the widespread evidence for the monumentalisation of the town's public spaces in the second century BC. Stratigraphic investigations by Maiuri in the 1940s and by Paul Arthur in the 1980s resulted in a clear picture of the monumentalisation of the Forum in this period. It is not necessarily the case that the types of activities within the Forum area changed radically, but they now took place in a much more monumentally impressive setting. Previously the Forum had consisted of an open space of beaten earth, with the Temple of Apollo on one side, and a line of shops on the other, providing a simple setting for everyday commercial transactions. Similarly, evidence for religious activity emerges before the Temple of Jupiter itself was built, since a pit containing votive deposits (including pots, bronze coins, architectural terracotta fragments, statuettes, and iron objects) probably dating from the late third century BC was uncovered next to the place where the altar of the Temple of Jupiter was later situated.[47]

During the second century BC all this changed: the Forum's piazza was paved in grey tufa blocks and was surrounded by a portico, and the Basilica and Temple of Jupiter were constructed.[48] The *macellum* seen today was also preceded by a market building built during the latter half of the second century BC, albeit on a different design. Instead of including a circular structure in the centre of a piazza, it comprised an uncovered area surrounded by a portico, with a series of shop units.[49] This extensive transformation of the Forum impacted on the adjacent Temple of Apollo too, since the construction of the portico around the main piazza followed its new orientation, encroaching upon the sanctuary. This required the building of a new enclosure wall for the sanctuary, whose irregularity was disguised by gradually increasing the thickness of the line of pilasters going from south to north.[50] Some space belonging to the sanctuary was lost in this way, and it seems that the cessation of ritual activities in this particular area was formalised by sealing up deposits of votive materials during the second half of the second century BC. These deposits provide clear evidence of Pompeii's openness to the outside world in the preceding period and help to explain how such large-scale building projects could be funded at this time. They include Megarian, Ampuritana, and Iberian ware, *amphorae* from Rhodes and Tunisia, and over a hundred bronze coins from Ebusus on the Balearic Islands.[51] At the same time, although the sanctuary area was reduced in size, the temple itself experienced a grand architectural transformation from a wooden structure into an impressive hellenistic-style stone building.[52]

Nor was the Forum the only public area to be transformed, but also the area adjacent to the 'Triangular Forum' district came to be occupied by the large Theatre, 'Samnite' Palaestra, and Temple of Isis. At the same time, the first monumental inscriptions from Pompeii written in Oscan allow us to gain some appreciation of the town's political structure (with its assembly and council), the role of magistrates in sponsoring public buildings, and the impact of hellenistic culture upon the town's religious life, not least with the construction of a suburban sanctuary to Dionysus.[53] This sanctuary, which is under a kilometre outside Pompeii to the south of the

Amphitheatre, was suddenly revealed by a rather more drastic type of probing beneath the surface than that carried out by archaeologists. Its discovery was the result of a bomb dropped by the allied forces in 1943. The sanctuary appears to have originated in the second half of the third century BC, and to have continued in use until AD 79.[54] Oscan inscriptions on its altar and on the ramp leading up into the temple itself show that the cult was introduced officially by the town's magistrates, although the sanctuary's location outside the town's walls may indicate that the cult was regarded as somewhat foreign and exotic at the time.[55] The discovery of the tufa pediment, depicting Dionysus himself holding a bunch of grapes and a wine cup, together with other figures commonly associated with him (such as a panther) and a female figure who has been variously interpreted as Ariadne or Aphrodite, has allowed the cult to be securely identified.[56] The decree of the Roman Senate in 186 BC restricting the celebration of Dionysian rites, which was designed to curtail the cult not just in Rome but among Rome's Italian allies too, of whom Pompeii was one at this time as part of the Nucerian League, apparently had no impact upon this sanctuary, since there is no sign of disruption in the archaeological record.[57] This perhaps suggests that the Oscan-speaking Samnites of Pompeii were keen to maintain this hellenistic cult, despite Rome's disapproval, and may be an indication of how deeply culture and society in Pompeii were influenced by hellenistic traditions during the second century BC.

This great boom in the town's prosperity and its impact upon its urban development is something which Pompeii shared with other towns in Campania, and it appears to be at least in part the result of increased trading connections with the Greek East, especially Delos.[58] For this stage in the town's development, surface remains alongside subsoil investigations are a much more valid form of evidence than for the town's earlier phases. By way of an example, we may take the case of the 'House of the Faun' (VI.xii.2). What the visitor sees today essentially reflects the house's grandiose transformation during the second century BC. It was designed to impress the visitor right from its entrance-passageway, with its multi-coloured stucco miniature shrines above the visitor's head, and its magnificent vista through the *atrium* into the two peristyles beyond.[59] Two-thirds of its ground-floor was devoted to reception areas, and it is hard to imagine that any viewer would have failed to be filled with admiration at the lavish 'Alexander mosaic' (made up of over one and a half million tiny *tesserae*, or coloured cubes), whose position allowed it to be viewed from both peristyles. It seems likely that the mosaic's hellenistic theme – the battle between Alexander the Great and the Persian king Darius – reflects the owner's cultural allegiances, although its framing by Nilotic scenes may suggest that the hellenistic model came to Pompeii via Alexandria rather than directly from the Greek East. We do not know who inhabited this residence, which rivals hellenistic palaces in its scale and grandeur, but it reflects the prosperity and hellenistic tastes not only of its owner but also of the town as a whole during this period.[60]

Although, therefore, recent stratigraphic digs have probed deep beneath the archaeological surface, there is still much left to probe historically by further excavation. As this chapter has demonstrated, much more work needs to be done in order to reveal the town's pre-Roman history. In particular, very little is yet known about the period from the fifth to the third centuries BC. Although some aspects of Pompeii's early history, such as the presence of Etruscans, now seem to be confirmed, our picture of archaic Pompeii remains a tantalising series of contradictory glimpses into a settlement whose appearance changes almost each time archaeologists start to dig down.

Notes

Introduction

1. J.W. von Goethe, *Italian Journey* (*The Collected Works* VI, trans. R.R. Heitner, with introduction and notes by T.P. Saine, ed. T.P. Saine & J.L. Sammons) (Princeton, NJ: Princeton University Press, 1989) 167.

1. Prologue to the Nightmare

1. Livy 9.38.2-3.

2. Appian, *Civil Wars* 1.39; Velleius Paterculus 2.16.2.

3. Cicero, *Speech in defence of Sulla* 60-2.

4. Seneca and Tacitus give different consular dates for the earthquake, but Onorato, 'La data del terremoto di Pompei' (1949), argued strongly that the earthquake struck in AD 62, not AD 63, and this is now generally accepted to be the case. Hine, 'The date of the Campanian earthquake' (1984) provides a more recent exploration of the discrepancies between the two authors.

5. J. Ginsburg, *Tradition and Theme in the Annals of Tacitus* (Salem, NH: The Ayer Company, 1981) ch. 3, on such sections.

6. Ling, *The Insula of the Menander* (1997) 15.

7. For detailed discussion of repair work in the town, see Adam, 'Observations techniques sur les suites du séisme' (1986) especially 72-6.

8. S.C. Nappo, 'L'impianto idrico a Pompei nel 79 d.C.. Nuovi dati', in *Cura Aquarum in Campania. Proceedings of the Ninth International Congress on the History of Water Management and Hydraulic Engineering in the Mediterranean Region*, ed. N. de Haan & G.C.M. Jansen (Leiden: Babesch supplement no. 4, 1996) 37-45; and 'Evidenze di danni strutturali, restauri e rifacimenti nelle insulae gravitanti su via Nocera a Pompei', in *Archäologie und Seismologie* (1995) 45-55, at 51-2.

9. 'House of the Chaste Lovers': A. Varone, 'Più terremoti a Pompei? I nuovi dati degli scavi di via dell'Abbondanza', in *Archäologie und Seismologie* (1995) 29-35; S.C. Nappo, *Pompeii. Guide to the Lost City* (London: Weidenfeld & Nicolson, 1998) 56-8. Compare the complex picture in I.ix.11-12, where commercial activity was apparently taking place in far from pristine conditions: J. Berry, 'The conditions of domestic life in Pompeii in AD 79: a case-study of Houses 11 and 12, Insula 9, Region 1', *Papers of the British School at Rome* 52 (1997) 103-25.

10. Adam, 'Observations techniques sur les suites du séisme' (1986) 76, 74.

11. *Archäologie und Seismologie* (1995) presents the proceedings of a conference devoted to re-examining archaeological evidence in the light of recent work by seismologists and vulcanologists.

12. Maiuri, *L'ultima fase edilizia di Pompei* (1942) 74-5.

13. Adam, 'Observations techniques sur les suites du séisme' (1986) 76; L. Jacobelli, 'I terremoti fra il 62 e il 79 nell'area vesuviana: le ragioni di un convegno', in *Archäologie und Seismologie* (1995) 17-21, at 17.

14. U. Pappalardo, 'L'eruzione pliniana del Vesuvio nel 79 d.C.: Ercolano', in *Volcanologie et Archéologie* (Strasbourg: PACT 25, 1990) 197-215, at 209.

15. Ling, *The Insula of the Menander* (1997) 18, 88, 236-7.

16. A. De Simone, 'I terremoti precedenti l'eruzione. Nuove attestazione da recenti scavi', in *Archäologie und Seismologie* (1995) 37-43, at 39.

17. A. & M. de Vos, *Pompei, Ercolano, Stabia* (Rome & Bari: Guide archeologiche Laterza, 1988) 110; illustrated in J. Ward-Perkins & A. Claridge, *Pompeii AD 79* (London: Exhibition catalogue, Royal Academy of Arts, 1976) 57.

18. A. & M. de Vos, *Pompei, Ercolano, Stabia* (Rome & Bari: Guide archeologiche Laterza, 1988) 102-4; S. Nappo, *Pompeii. Guide to the Lost City* (London: Weidenfeld & Nicolson, 1998) 59-61. Electoral notice: *Corpus Inscriptionum Latinarum* IV 7164.

19. Maiuri, *L'ultima fase edilizia di Pompei* (1942) 217, with comments on the 'House of the Menander' at 152; critique by A. Wallace-Hadrill, 'Elites and trade in the Roman town', in *City and Country in the Ancient World*, ed. J. Rich & A. Wallace-Hadrill (London & NY: Routledge, 1991) 241-72, especially at 251-3. Maiuri's overall picture is still adopted by P. Zanker, *Pompeji. Stadtbilder als Spiegel von Gesellschaft und Herrschaftsform* (Mainz, Trierer Winckelmannsprogramme 9: 1987) 42.

20. M. De' Spagnolis Conticello, 'Sul rinvenimento della villa e del monumento funerario dei Lucretii Valentes', *Rivista di studi pompeiani* 6 (1993-4) 147-66.

21. II.iii.3, 'House of Marine Venus': M. Della Corte, *Case ed abitanti di Pompei*, 2nd edn (Rome: «L'Erma» di Bretschneider, 1954) 321, and 3rd edn, ed. P. Soprano (Naples: Fausto Fiorentino editore, 1965) 383-6, M. Della Corte, 'X. Pompei. Iscrizioni scoperte nel quinquennio 1951-1956', *Notizie degli Scavi* (1958) 77-184, at 91-2, nos 64-5 and *Corpus Inscriptionum Latinarum* IV 9888-9 for the graffiti. For comments on the confusion surrounding Della Corte's identifications, see H.B. Van der Poel, *Corpus Topographicum Pompeianum* II. *Toponymy* (Rome: University of Texas at Austin, 1983) 101-2, 235 with n. 2, 239 with n. 2. The family has been discussed most recently by J.L. Franklin, jr., *Pompeis Difficile Est. Studies in the Political Life of Imperial Pompeii* (Ann Arbor: University of Michigan Press, 2001) 101-6.

22. H. Mouritsen, *Elections, Magistrates and Municipal Élite. Studies in Pompeian Epigraphy* (Rome: «L'Erma» di Bretschneider, 1988) 35.

23. Adam, 'Observations techniques sur les suites du séisme' (1986) 83. For a recent re-statement that many of the workshops are post-62, see A. Meneghini, 'Trasformazione di una residenza domestica in impianto commerciale a Pompei: l'esempio della bottega I.11.1,2', *Rivista di studi pompeiani* 10 (1999) 11-22.

24. Andreau, 'Histoire des séismes et histoire économique' (1973) 388.

25. R.I. Curtis, 'The garum shop of Pompeii', *Cronache pompeiane* 5 (1979) 5-23.

26. J. Berry, 'Household artefacts: towards a reinterpretation of Roman domestic space', in *Domestic Space in the Roman World: Pompeii and Beyond*, ed. R.

Laurence & A. Wallace-Hadrill (Portsmouth, RI: *Journal of Roman Archaeology* supplement 22, 1997) 183-95.

27. F. Pirson, 'Rented accommodation at Pompeii: the evidence of the *Insula Arriana Polliana* VI 6', in *Domestic Space in the Roman World: Pompeii and Beyond*, ed. R. Laurence & A. Wallace-Hadrill (Portsmouth, RI: *Journal of Roman Archaeology* supplement 22, 1997) 165-81; H. Parkins, 'The "consumer city" domesticated? The Roman city in élite economic strategies', in *Roman Urbanism Beyond the Consumer City*, ed. H.M. Parkins (London & NY: Routledge, 1997) 83-111.

28. *Corpus Inscriptionum Latinarum* X 846.

29. H. Mouritsen, 'Mobility and social change in Italian towns during the principate', in *Roman Urbanism Beyond the Consumer City*, ed. H.M. Parkins (London & NY: Routledge, 1997) 59-82, at 65-70; 'Order and disorder in Pompeian politics', in *Les élites municipales de l'Italie péninsulaire des Gracques à Néron*, ed. M. Cébeillac-Gervasoni (Naples & Rome: Collection Centre Jean Bérard 13/Collection École Française de Rome 215, 1996) 139-44.

30. J. Andreau, 'Remarques sur la société pompéienne (à propos des tablettes de L. Caecilius Jucundus', *Dialoghi di archeologia* 7 (1973) 213-54, especially at 217.

31. Allison, 'Artefact assemblages' (1992). She has explored these ideas in several publications: see further reading.

32. *Corpus Inscriptionum Latinarum* X 810 and 959.

33. J. Berry, 'Household artefacts: towards a re-interpretation of Roman domestic space', in *Domestic Space in the Roman World: Pompeii and Beyond*, ed. R. Laurence & A. Wallace-Hadrill (Portsmouth, RI: *Journal of Roman Archaeology* supplement 22, 1997) 184, fig. 1.

34. J. Berry, 'Household artefacts: towards a reinterpretation of Roman domestic space', in *Domestic Space in the Roman World: Pompeii and Beyond*, ed. R. Laurence & A. Wallace-Hadrill (Portsmouth, RI: *Journal of Roman Archaeology* supplement 22, 1997) 183-95.

35. L. Nevett, 'Perceptions of domestic space in Roman Italy', in *The Roman Family in Italy: Status, Sentiment, Space*, ed. B. Rawson & P.R.C. Weaver (Canberra & Oxford: Humanities Research Centre & Clarendon Press, 1997) 281-98.

36. *Corpus Inscriptionum Latinarum* X 1018; discussed by M. Della Corte, 'Il pomerium di Pompei', *Rendiconti dell'Accademia Nazionale dei Lincei. Classe di scienze morali, storiche e filologiche* ser. 5 vol. 22 (1913) 261-308.

37. Maiuri, *L'ultima fase edilizia di Pompei* (1942) 211.

38. For this broad historical context, see M. Griffin, 'The Flavians', in *The Cambridge Ancient History* XI. *The High Empire AD 70-192*, ed. A.K. Bowman, P. Garnsey, D. Rathbone (Cambridge: Cambridge University Press, 2nd edn, 2000) 1-83, at 29-31. The inscriptions from elsewhere include *Année Épigraphique* (1945) 85, Cannes, *Inscriptiones Latinae Selectae* 5955, Bou-Arada, North Africa, and *Inscriptiones Latinae Selectae* 251, Capua.

39. Adam, 'Observations techniques sur les suites du séisme' (1986) 86; P. Zanker, *Pompeji. Stadtbilder als Spiegel von Gesellschaft und Herrschaftsform* (Mainz, Trierer Winckelmannsprogramme 9: 1987) 41.

40. Andreau, 'Il terremoto del 62' (1984) 42.

41. P. Zanker, *Pompeji. Stadtbilder als Spiegel von Gesellschaft und*

Herrschaftsform (Mainz, Trierer Winckelmannsprogramme 9: 1987) 41-2; Andreau, 'Histoire de séismes et histoire économique' (1973) 389.

42. Mau, 'Il portico del foro' (1891).

43. Mau, *Pompeii* (1899) 63. This idea was repeated more recently by H. Döhl & P. Zanker, 'La scultura', in *Pompei 79*, ed. F. Zevi (Naples: Gaetano Macchiaroli editore, 1984) 177-210 at 182, with 180 fig. 92a, 181 fig. 92b.

44. This was suggested tentatively by A.W. Van Buren, 'Studies in the archaeology of the Forum at Pompeii', *Memoirs of the American Academy in Rome* 2 (1918) 67-76, at 68-70, and argued fully by H.G. Martin, *Römische Tempelkultbilder. Eine archäologische Untersuchung zur späten Republik* (Rome: Studi e materiali del Museo della civiltà romana no.12, «L'Erma» di Bretschneider, 1987) 222-3, Kat. 9 with plates 21-2. I am grateful to Bert Smith for advice on this point.

45. *Corpus Inscriptionum Latinarum* X 796-7.

46. D. Russo, *Il tempio di Giove Meilichio a Pompei* (Naples: Accademia di archeologia, lettere e belle arti di Napoli, Monumenti no. 8, 1991) chs 7-8; P. Zanker, *Pompeji. Stadtbilder als Spiegel von Gesellschaft und Herrschaftsform* (Mainz, Trierer Winckelmannsprogramme 9: 1987) 41.

47. S. De Caro, 'La città sannitica urbanistica e architettura', in *Pompei* I, ed. F. Zevi (Naples: Banco di Napoli, 1991) 23-46, at 41-2.

48. Dobbins, 'Problems of chronology' (1994). Compare Wallat, 'Der Zustand des Forums von Pompeji', in *Archäologie und Seismologie* (1995).

49. Andreau, 'Il terremoto del 62' (1984) 42.

50. Fiorelli, *Pompeianarum Antiquitatum Historia* I (1860) part 3, 139, 15 and 19 Dec. 1813; 143, 10 Feb. 1814; 145, 6 Mar. 1814.

51. Fiorelli, *Pompeianarum Antiquitatum Historia* I (1860) Part 3 Addenda, 'Supplementum ex codice Ribaviano' 225 – marble statue; I (1860) part 3, 187, 4 Jan. 1817 – bronze fragments.

52. Fiorelli, *Pompeianarum Antiquitatum Historia* I (1860) part 3, 193, 19 June, and 195, 12 July 1817.

53. Fiorelli, *Pompeianarum Antiquitatum Historia* I (1860) part 3, 195-6, 15 July 1817.

54. Fiorelli, *Pompeianarum Antiquitatum Historia* II (1862) part 4, 21, 6 May 1820.

55. Fiorelli, *Pompeianarum Antiquitatum Historia* I (1860) part 3, 159, 25 Aug. 1814.

56. Fiorelli, *Pompeianarum Antiquitatum Historia* II (1862) part 4, 14, 15 Jan. 1820.

2. The Nightmare Revealed

1. F. Dobran, A. Neri & M. Todesco, 'Assessing the pyroclastic flow hazard at Vesuvius', *Nature* 367 (1994) 551-4, at 551.

2. R. Trevelyan (himself involved in the allied military expedition to Italy), *The Shadow of Vesuvius*, ch. 1 (London: The Folio Society, 1976) sketches a vivid picture of the 1944 eruption, drawing on eye-witness statements and capturing the atmosphere of the time.

3. A vivid account of the eruption of Mount Pelée can be found in *Planet Earth*.

Volcano, ed. T.A. Lewis (Amsterdam: Time-Life Books, 1982) ch. 1. The relevance of Mount Pelée for understanding Vesuvius was noted early on in two articles by E.T. Merrill, 'Notes on the eruption of Vesuvius in 79 AD', *American Journal of Archaeology* 22 (1918) 304-9, and 'Further note on the eruption of Vesuvius in 79 AD', *American Journal of Archaeology* 24 (1920) 262-8, but did not attract much agreement. Many of Merrill's acute observations have only recently been vindicated by Sparks, 'Dusts of destruction' (1973) 134 and Sigurdsson, Cashdollar, Sparks, 'The eruption of Vesuvius in AD 79' (1982) 41.

4. L. Breglia, 'Circolazione monetale ed aspetti di vita economica a Pompei', in *Pompeiana. Raccolta di studi per il secondo centenario degli scavi di Pompei* (Naples: Gaetano Macchiaroli editore, 1950) 41-59, with tables showing circumstances of coin-finds, where known.

5. Attempts to argue that the eruption occurred in November rather than in August have not gained support, and have most recently been refuted by A. Ciarallo & E. De Carolis, 'La data dell'eruzione', *Rivista di studi pompeiani* 9 (1998) 63-73.

6. Sigurdsson, Cashdollar, Sparks, 'The eruption of Vesuvius in AD 79' (1982), 44-50 and Scandone, Giacomelli, Gasparini, 'Mount Vesuvius' (1993) 6-8 assess the value of Pliny's letters as evidence for the eruption.

7. R. Cioni, P. Marianelli, R. Santacroce, A. Sbrana, 'Plinian and subplinian eruptions', in *Encyclopedia of Volcanoes* (2000) 477-94, at 486.

8. Sparks, 'Dusts of destruction' (1973), 135. A recent technical summary of the eruption is provided by R. Cioni, P. Marianelli, R. Santacroce, A. Sbrana, 'Plinian and subplinian eruptions', in *Encyclopedia of Volcanoes* (2000) 477-94, at 485-6.

9. R. Findley, 'Eruption of Mount St Helens', *National Geographic Magazine* vol. 159 no.1 (January 1981) 3-65, at 7, 17.

10. Carey & Sigurdsson, 'Temporal variations in column height' (1987).

11. Sigurdsson, Cashdollar, Sparks, 'The eruption of Vesuvius in AD 79' (1982), 48; Papale & Dobran, 'Modeling of the ascent of magma' (1993) 101; Scandone, 'I meccanismi eruttivi' (1995), another overall account of the eruption.

12. Luongo, Perrotta, Scarpati, 'The eruption of AD 79' (1999) 32.

13. Varone & Marturano, 'L'eruzione vesuviana' (1997) 59, 61.

14. Sigurdsson, Cashdollar, Sparks, 'The eruption of Vesuvius in AD 79' (1982) 48.

15. M. Della Corte, 'I. Pompei. Scavo della 'Grande Palestra' nel quartiere dell'Anfiteatro', *Notizie degli scavi* (1939) 165-327, at 227.

16. G. Fiorelli, *Pompeianarum Antiquitatum Historia* I (Naples: 1860) part 3, 203, 5th May 1818.

17. Varone & Marturano, 'L'eruzione vesuviana' (1997) 62.

18. Carey & Sigurdsson, 'Temporal variations in column height' (1987) 303; Papale & Dobran, 'Modeling of the ascent of magma' (1993) 101.

19. Varone & Marturano, 'L'eruzione vesuviana' (1997) 60.

20. Carey & Sigurdsson, 'Temporal variations in column height' (1987) 303.

21. Definitions taken from Sparks, 'Dusts of destruction' (1973) 135; see also Luongo, Perrotta, Scarpati, 'The eruption of AD 79' (1999) 31.

22. Varone & Marturano, 'L'eruzione vesuviana' (1997) 66.

23. Sigurdsson, Cashdollar, Sparks, 'The eruption of Vesuvius in AD 79' (1982)

41, 49; *Planet Earth. Volcano*, ed. T.A. Lewis (Amsterdam: Time-Life Books, 1982) 32.

24. Sparks, 'Dusts of destruction' (1973) 135-6.

25. Sigurdsson, Cashdollar, Sparks, 'The eruption of Vesuvius in AD 79' (1982) 43.

26. Pappalardo, 'L'eruzione pliniana' (1990) 198, with n. 6.

27. R. Gore & O.L. Massatenta, 'The Dead do tell Tales', *National Geographic Magazine* 265 (1984) 557-613; S.C. Bisel, 'Human bones at Herculaneum', *Rivista di studi pompeiani* 1 (1987) 123-9; M. Pagano, 'Gli scheletri dei fuggiaschi di Ercolano: l'indagine archeologica', 39-41 & G. Mastrolorenzo & P.P. Petrone, 'Studi scientifici sull'eruzione e i suoi effetti', 51-9 – both in *Gli antichi ercolanesi. Antropologia, società, economica*, ed. M. Pagano (Naples: Electa Napoli, 2000). The new evidence from Herculaneum is also clearly presented for children in S.C. Bisel, *The Secrets of Vesuvius* (Sevenoaks: Hodder & Stoughton/Madison Press, 1990).

28. Pappalardo, 'L'eruzione pliniana' (1990) 199; M. Pagano, 'Iscrizione della statua di Marco Nonio Balbo posta davanti alle Terme Suburbane', *Rivista di studi pompeiani* 2 (1988) 238-9; A. Maiuri, 'Un decreto onorario di M. Nonio Balbo scoperto recentemente ad Ercolano', *Reale Accademia d'Italia, Rendiconti* ser.7, vol. 3, fasc.12 (1942) 253-78.

29. Sigurdsson, Cashdollar, Sparks, 'The eruption of Vesuvius in AD 79' (1982) 43; Pappalardo, 'L'eruzione pliniana' (1990); Kent, Ninkovich, Pescatore, Sparks, 'Palaeomagnetic determination of emplacement temperature' (1981).

30. For this sequence, see Pescatore & Sigurdsson, 'L'eruzione del Vesuvio' (1993) 453.

31. Varone & Marturano, 'L'eruzione vesuviana' (1997) 69.

32. De Carolis, Patricelli, Ciarallo, 'Rinvenimenti di corpi umani' (1998) especially 78-113; Pescatore & Sigurdsson, 'L'eruzione del Vesuvio' (1993) 451.

33. Varone & Marturano, 'L'eruzione vesuviana' (1997) 70.

34. Sigurdsson, Cashdollar, Sparks, 'The eruption of Vesuvius in AD 79' (1982) 49.

35. De Carolis, Patricelli, Ciarallo, 'Rinvenimenti di corpi umani' (1998) especially 78-113.

36. Varone & Marturano, 'L'eruzione vesuviana' (1997) 62-5.

37. Varone & Marturano, 'L'eruzione vesuviana' (1997) 58.

38. A. Maiuri, 'Gli scavi di Pompei dal 1879 al 1948', in *Pompeiana. Raccolta di studi per il secondo centenario degli scavi di Pompei* (Naples: Gaetano Macchiaroli editore, 1950) 9-40, at 14.

39. Sigurdsson, *Melting the Earth* (1999), at 70.

3. A Broken Sleep

1. Celsinus' funerary inscription: F. Marco Simón, 'Las estelas decoradas de los conventos Caesaraugustano y Cluniense', *Caesaraugusta: Publicaciones del Seminario de Arqueología y Numismática Aragonesas* 43-4 (1978) 122 no. B16. I am grateful to Fiona Rose for drawing my attention to this inscription, and to Olli Salomies for advice on this nomenclature. The Popidii at Pompeii: P. Castrén, *Ordo Populusque Pompeianus. Polity and Society in Roman Pompeii* (Rome: Bardi editore, 1975) no. 318. Temple of Isis inscription: *Corpus Inscriptionum Latinarum* X 846. I am suspicious about the authenticity of the *stele* not only because no photograph has ever been published of it and it is now lost, but also because it fits so nicely with our Pompeian evidence, even down to mentioning the fact that Popidius Celsinus was a town councillor (*decurio*), also commemorated in the Pompeian building inscription. His 'son's' name also appears rather odd. Furthermore, the text does not seem to fit well with the military relief sculpted above it: similar reliefs from this area accompany texts clearly belonging to soldiers. I wonder whether the inscription has been added to an authentic grave marker, but reserve judgement without seeing the object itself.

2. K.M. Coleman, *Statius Silvae IV* (Oxford: Clarendon Press, 1988) 209 and *Prosopographia Imperi Romani*[2] Pars IV, ed. A. Stein & L. Petersen (Berlin: De Gruyter, 1952-66) I no. 430 for Julius Menecrates.

3. L. Bosio, *La Tabula Peutingeriana. Una descrizione pittorica del mondo antico* (Rimini: Maggioli, Monumenti dell'arte classica 2, 1983) 102, fig. 31. See now too the recent observations on the complex chronological layers of the *tabula* by B. Salway, 'Travel, *itineraria* and *tabellaria*', in *Travel and Geography in the Roman Empire*, ed. C. Adams & R. Laurence (London & NY: Routledge, 2001) 22-66, especially at 22-6, 44, 58. I am grateful to Richard Talbert for discussing this issue with me.

4. A. Maiuri, *Pompeii* (Rome: Istituto geografico de Agostini, 1929) 7.

5. Dio Cassius 66.24.3-4; Suetonius, *Life of Titus* 8.4.

6. *Corpus Inscriptionum Latinarum* X 1481, *Année Épigraphique* (1902) 40.

7. Descoeudres, 'Did some Pompeians return?' (1993) 169-71; Zevi, 'Sul Tempio di Iside' (1994) 51-6; Cerulli Irelli, 'Intorno al problema della rinascita' (1975) 295-6. Such holes are clearly illustrated in the 'House of the Menander': A. Maiuri, *La Casa del Menandro e il suo tesoro di argenteria* (Rome: La libreria dello stato, 1932) 175, fig. 83. Disturbance from tunnelling was recently documented in I.ix.12, room 4: J. Berry, 'The conditions of domestic life in Pompeii in AD 79: a case-study of Houses 11 and 12, Insula 9, Region 1', *Papers of the British School at Rome* 52 (1997) 103-25, at 112, 118.

8. A. & M. de Vos, *Pompei, Ercolano, Stabia* (Rome & Bari: Guide archeologiche Laterza, 1982) 192; *Corpus Inscriptionum Latinarum* IV 2311.

9. C. Bonucci, *Pompei descritta* (Naples: R. Miranda, 1827 3rd edn) 33.

10. J.J. Winckelmann, *Lettre à M. le Comte de Brühl. Sur les découvertes d'Herculanum* (Dresden 1764: French translation from original German of 1762) 15. On the moving about of late antique statues, compare C. Lepelley, 'Le musée des statues divines. La volonté de sauvegarder le patrimoine artistique païen à l'époque théodosienne', *Cahiers Archéologiques* 42 (1994) 5-15.

11. A. Maiuri, *La Casa del Menandro e il suo tesoro di argenteria* (Rome: La libreria dello stato, 1932) 176; R. Ling, *The Insula of the Menander at Pompeii. I. The Structures* (Oxford: Oxford University Press, 1997) 10.

12. A. Varone & A. Marturano, 'L'eruzione vesuviana del 24 agosto del 79 d.C. attraverso le lettere di Plinio il Giovane e le nuove evidenze archeologiche', *Rivista di studi pompeiani* 8 (1997) 57-72, at 65.

13. R. Ling, *The Insula of the Menander at Pompeii. I. The Structures* (Oxford: Oxford University Press, 1997) 11.

14. Cerulli Irelli, 'Intorno al problema della rinascita di Pompei' (1975) 295, 298.

15. A.K. Ostrow, *The Sarno Bath Complex* (Rome: Soprintendenza archeologica di Pompei, Monografie 4, «L'Erma» di Bretschneider, 1990) 40.

16. M. De' Spagnolis Conticello, 'Sul rinvenimento della villa e del monumento funerario dei Lucretii Valentes', *Rivista di studi pompeiani* 6 (1993-4) 147-66, at 147.

17. *Pacien de Barcelone, Écrits*, with introduction, critical text & commentary by C. Granado (Paris: Les éditions du Cerf: Sources Chrétiennes no. 410, 1995) *Sermo de paenitentibus* 11.5-6. I am grateful to Christine Rauer for help with this text.

18. Alagi, 'La zona vesuviana' (1971) made some observations along these lines.

19. R. Findley, 'Eruption of Mount St Helens', *National Geographic Magazine* vol. 159 no.1 (January 1981) 3-65, at 12-13, 62.

20. I.W.B. Thornton, 'The ecology of volcanoes: recovery and reassembly of living communities', in *Encyclopedia of Volcanoes*, ed. H. Sigurdsson (San Diego: Academic Press, 2000) 1057-81, at 1061-2.

21. R. Findley, 'Eruption of Mount St Helens', *National Geographic Magazine* vol. 159 no.1 (January 1981) 3-65, at 62.

22. For various approaches to this question, see Pagano, 'L'area vesuviana' (1995-6); De Carolis, 'Testimonianze archeologiche' (1997); Soricelli, 'La regione vesuviana' (1997); De Carolis, 'Rinvenimenti di tombe' (1998).

23. Sogliano, 'La rinascita di Pompei' (1915) 485, 502-3, with comments of Maiuri, 'Gli scavi di Pompei' (1950) 21 and Castiglione Morelli del Franco, 'Il Giornale dei Soprastanti' (1993) 663. The area is marked on Pagano, 'L'area vesuviana' (1995-96) fig. 1, no. 30.

24. E. De Carolis, 'Pompei-Suburbio. Comune di Pompei. Via Lepanto', *Rivista di studi pompeiani* 3 (1989) 245-7; Pagano, 'L'area vesuviana' (1995-6) 38; Soricelli, 'La regione vesuviana' (1997) 145-6.

25. Pagano, 'L'area vesuviana' (1995-6) fig. 1, no. 31.

26. M. de' Spagnolis Conticello, *Il Pons Sarni di Scafati e la via Nuceria-Pompeios* (Rome: Soprintendenza archeologica di Pompei, Monografie 8, «L'Erma» di Bretschneider, 1994) 53, 78, 94-6 argues that a road was put in place above the one destroyed in the eruption more or less immediately afterwards.

27. Milestones: *Corpus Inscriptionum Latinarum* X 6940, 6939. Road-building: Pagano, 'L'area vesuviana' (1995-6) 37-8; Soricelli, 'La regione vesuviana' (1997) 139; De Carolis, 'Testimonianze archeologiche' (1997) 24.

28. As Pagano, 'L'area vesuviana' (1995-6) 37 suggests.

29. A. Desbat & H. Savay-Guerraz, 'Note sur la découverte d'amphores Dressel 2/4 italiques, tardives, à Saint-Romain-en-Gal (Rhône)' *Gallia* 47 (1990) 203-11; Soricelli, 'La regione vesuviana' (1997) 146-7.

30. Russo, *Il tempio di Giove Meilichio a Pompei* (1991), ch. 3; the inscriptions are *Corpus Inscriptionum Latinarum* X 928, 952.

31. Kidwell, *Sannazaro and Arcadia* (1993) 101.

32. Kidwell, *Sannazaro and Arcadia* (1993) 45.

33. Kidwell, *Sannazaro and Arcadia* (1993) 111-12.

34. Kidwell, *Sannazaro and Arcadia* (1993) 135-6.

35. Bowersock, 'The rediscovery of Herculaneum and Pompeii' (1978) 464.

36. G. Fiorelli, *Pompei. Illustrazione de' monumenti* (Naples, Stamperia dell'Iride, 1851) viii; Bowersock, 'The rediscovery of Herculaneum and Pompeii' (1978) 464.

37. G. Fiorelli, *Pompei. Illustrazione de' monumenti* (Naples, Stamperia dell'Iride, 1851) i.

38. J. Winckelmann, *Lettre à M. le Comte de Brühl. Sur les découvertes d'Herculanum* (Dresden 1764, French translation from original German of 1762) 19.

39. Latapie, 'Description des fouilles de Pompéii (a.1776)', (1953) at 226, 233-4; see also L. Mascoli & G. Vallet, 'Le dialogue des sciences de la nature et de l'archéologie au moment des découvertes d'Herculanum et de Pompéi', in *Ercolano 1738-1988. 250 anni di ricerca archeologica* ed. F. Franchi dell'Orto (Rome: «L'Erma» di Bretschneider, 1993) 429-37.

4. The Reawakening

1. *Recueil d'Antiquités Égyptiennes, Étrusques, Grècques, Romaines et Gauloises* III (Paris: Desaint & Saillant, 1759) 143; Allroggen-Bedel, 'Archäologie und Politik' (1996) 223.

2. For this political background, see Carpanetto, 'Bourbon Italy: Naples and Parma' (1987) at 179; Acton, *The Bourbons of Naples* (1957) ch. 1.

3. De Caro, *The National Archaeological Museum of Naples* (1996) 11.

4. T. Bauman, 'The eighteenth century: serious opera', in *The Oxford Illustrated History of Opera*, ed. R. Parker (Oxford & NY: Oxford University Press, 1994) 47-83, at 53.

5. Oresko, 'Culture in the age of baroque and rococo' (1997) at 160-1.

6. G. Hanlon, *Early Modern Italy, 1550-1800. Three Seasons in European History* (Basingstoke & London: Macmillan, European Studies Series, 2000) 340.

7. Louis XIV: T. Carter, 'The seventeenth century', 1-46, at 35, and R. Savage, 'The staging of opera', 350-420, at 367; Teatro di San Carlo: T. Bauman, 'The eighteenth century: serious opera', 47-83, at 47, 50, and J. Rosselli, 'Opera as a social occasion', 450-82, at 461: all in *The Oxford Illustrated History of Opera*, ed. R. Parker (Oxford & NY: Oxford University Press, 1994).

8. Acton, *The Bourbons of Naples* (1957) 47-9, 77-81.

9. Oresko, 'Culture in the age of baroque and rococo' (1997) 160. The equestrian statue of Nonius Balbus *filius* is one of only five statues from Pompeii and Herculaneum which have been judged to have achieved the status of a 'classic' in taste: F. Haskell & N. Penny, *Taste and the Antique. The Lure of Classical Sculpture 1500-1900* (New Haven & London: Yale University Press, 1982); on the problems associated with these statues after cannon damage, and their porcelain copies, see S. Adamo Muscettola, 'Nuove letture borboniche: i Nonii Balbi e il Foro di Ercolano', *Prospettiva* 28 (1982) 2-16.

10. L.A. Scatozza Höricht, 'Gli studi archeologici: dall'antiquaria alla storia' in *La cultura classica a Napoli nell'ottocento* II (Naples: Pubblicazioni del Dipartimento di filologia classica dell'Università degli Studi di Napoli, 1987) 815-23, at 818.

11. M-N. Pinot de Villechenon, 'Lost and recreated Antiquity. The album of the *Peintures d'Herculanum*', in *Ercolano e Pompei. Gli affreschi nelle illustrazioni* *neoclassiche dell'album delle "Peintures d'Herculanum" conservato al Louvre* (Milan: Franco Maria Ricci, 2000) 72-7, at 76.

12. F. Haskell & N. Penny, *Taste and the Antique. The Lure of Classical Sculpture 1500-1900* (New Haven & London: Yale University Press, 1982) 66.

13. The gradual shifting of the Farnese collection is traced by I. Bignamini & I. Jenkins, 'The antique' in *Grand Tour*, ed. Wilton & Bignamini (1996) 203-5, at 203; Pozzi Paolini, 'Il Museo Archeologico Nazionale di Napoli' (1977) 127, 129, 135; F. Haskell & N. Penny, *Taste and the Antique. The Lure of Classical Sculpture 1500-1900* (New Haven & London: Yale University Press, 1982) 76-7.

14. Oresko, 'Culture in the age of baroque and rococo' (1997) 152.

15. De Caro, *The National Archaeological Museum of Naples* (1996) 13.

16. J.W. von Goethe, *Italian Journey* (trans. R.R. Heitner, 1989) 131: 16 January 1787; Pozzi Paolini, 'Il Museo Archeologico Nazionale di Napoli' (1977) 7.

17. H. Harder, *Le Président de Brosses et le voyage en Italie au dix-huitième siècle* (Geneva: Slatkine, Biblioteca del viaggio in Italia no.5, 1981) 85.

18. Allroggen-Bedel, 'Archäologie und Politik' (1996).

19. Acton, *The Bourbons of Naples* (1957) 144-5.

20. J. Winckelmann, *Lettre à M. le Comte de Brühl. Sur les découvertes d'Herculanum* (Dresden 1764, French translation from original German of 1762).

21. A. Schnapp, *The Discovery of the Past. The Origins of Archaeology* (London: British Museum, 1996) (trans. I. Kinnes & G. Varndell) 246.

22. I. Jenkins, 'Contemporary minds. Sir William Hamilton's affair with antiquity', in *Vases and Volcanoes*, ed. Jenkins & Sloan (1996) 40-64, at 42.

23. F. Latapie, 'Description des fouilles de Pompéii (a.1776)', with introduction by P. Barrière and notes by A. Maiuri, *Rendiconti della Accademia di archeologica, lettere e belle arti* n.s. 28 (1953) 223-48, at 244.

24. L. Fino, *Ercolano e Pompei: vedute neoclassiche e romantiche* (Naples: Electa Napoli, 1988) 18.

25. Allroggen-Bedel, 'Archäologie und Politik' (1996) 223. On the Vatican's policy, see I. Bignamini, 'Grand Tour: open issues', in *Grand Tour*, ed. Wilton & Bignamini (1996) 31-6, at 33.

26. Allroggen-Bedel, 'Archäologie und Politik' (1996) 230.

27. Grell, *Herculanum et Pompéi dans les récits des voyageurs français* (1982) 57.

28. Allroggen-Bedel, 'Archäologie und Politik' (1996) 233.

29. Pozzi Paolini, 'Il Museo Archeologico Nazionale di Napoli' (1977) 133.

30. F. Ley, *Voyage en Italie du Baron de Krüdener en 1786* (Paris: Fischbacher, 1983): 9 September 1786 visit to Portici: 144-5; the baron's background: 19-20.

31. *Voyage en Italie de M. l'Abbé Barthélemy* (Paris: F. Buisson, 1802) 77: Letter 13, 2 Feb. 1756.

32. J.W. von Goethe, *Italian Journey* (trans. R.R. Heitner, 1989) 173: 18 March 1787.

33. F. Latapie, 'Description des fouilles de Pompéii (a.1776)', with introduction by P. Barrière and notes by A. Maiuri, *Rendiconti della Accademia di archeologica, lettere e belle arti* n.s. 28 (1953) 223-48, at 234.

34. Grell, *Herculanum et Pompéi dans les récits des voyageurs français* (1982) 124.

35. *Le Antichità di Ercolano esposte* I (Naples: Stamperia Reale, 1757).

36. On the engraving's significance, see Allroggen-Bedel, 'Archäologie und Politik' (1996) 220.

37. M-N. Pinot de Villechenon, 'Lost and recreated Antiquity. The album of the *Peintures d'Herculanum'*, in *Ercolano e Pompei. Gli affreschi nelle illustrazioni neoclassiche dell'album delle "Peintures d'Herculanum" conservato al Louvre* (Milan: Franco Maria Ricci, 2000) 72-7, at 74; I. Jenkins, 'Contemporary minds. Sir William Hamilton's affair with antiquity', in *Vases and Volcanoes*, ed. Jenkins & Sloan (1996) 40-64, at 43.

38. K. Sloan, 'Observations on the Kingdom of Naples. William Hamilton's diplomatic career', in *Vases and Volcanoes*, ed. Jenkins & Sloan (1996) 24-39, at 27.

39. C. Hornsby, 'Introduction, or why travel?', in *The Impact of Italy: the Grand Tour and Beyond*, ed. C. Hornsby (London: British School at Rome, 2000) 1-25, at 16; Acton, *The Bourbons of Naples* (1957) 660.

40. L. Fino, *Ercolano e Pompei: vedute neoclassiche e romantiche* (Naples: Electa Napoli, 1988) 16, citing J. Moore, *Lettres d'un voyageur anglais sur la France, la Suisse, l'Allemagne et l'Italie* (Lausanne, 1782).

41. M. de la Roque, *Voyage d'un Amateur des Arts, en Flandre, dans les Pays-Bas, en Hollande, en France, en Savoye, en Italie, en Suisse, fait dans les années 1775-78* (Amsterdam, 1783) III, 60; Grell, *Herculanum et Pompéi dans les récits des voyageurs français* (1982) 57.

42. B. Tanucci, *Epistolario* IX, 179, cited by F. Strazzullo, *Alcubierre-Weber-Paderni: un difficile 'tandem' nello scavo di Ercolano-Pompei-Stabia* (Naples: Accademia di Archeologia, Lettere e Belle Arti, 1998) 58.

43. Grell, *Herculanum et Pompéi dans les récits des voyageurs français* (1982) 101, citing Abbé Gabriel Coyer, *Voyage d'Italie et de Hollande* (Paris, 1776-8) 233; Famine: Carpanetto, 'Enlightenment and reform' (1987) 236.

44. Grell, *Herculanum et Pompéi dans les récits des voyageurs français* (1982) 3.

45. J.W. von Goethe, *Italian Journey* (trans. R.R. Heitner, 1989) 162: 11 March 1787.

46. M. de la Roque, *Voyage d'un Amateur des Arts, en Flandre, dans les Pays-Bas, en Hollande, en France, en Savoye, en Italie, en Suisse, fait dans les années 1775-78* (Amsterdam, 1783) III, 63-4.

47. C. Dickens, *American Notes and Pictures from Italy* (first published 1846; Oxford: Oxford University Press, The Oxford Illustrated Dickens, 1987) 416.

48. De Caro, *Alla ricerca di Iside* (1992) 12.

49. Grell, *Herculanum et Pompéi dans les récits des voyageurs français* (1982) 59-60; De Caro, *Alla ricerca di Iside* (1992) 13, citing J. Lalande, *Voyage d'un Français en Italie, fait dans les années 1765-66* VII, 208 (1st edn, Paris, 1769) and VII 549 (2nd edn, Paris, 1786).

50. De Caro, *Alla ricerca di Iside* (1992) 4; *Grand Tour*, ed. Wilton & Bignamini (1996) 232.

51. Reproduced in De Caro, *Alla ricerca di Iside* (1992) 11 = the Abbé de Saint-Non, *Voyage Pittoresque, ou Description du Royaume de Naples et de Sicile* (Paris 1781-6) II tav. 75 bis.

52. For recent disquiet about implying too much uniformity in talking of the

'Grand Tour', see I. Bignamini, 'Grand Tour: open issues', in *Grand Tour*, ed. Wilton & Bignamini (1996) 31-6; F. Salmon, 'The impact of the archaeology of Rome on British architects and their work c.1750-1840', in *The Impact of Italy: the Grand Tour and Beyond*, ed. C. Hornsby (London: British School at Rome, 2000) 219-43, at 219.

53. Grell, *Herculanum et Pompéi dans les récits des voyageurs français* (1982) 5-8.

54. F. Ley, *Voyage en Italie du Baron de Krüdener en 1786* (Paris: Fischbacher, 1983) 38.

55. Bergeret de Grancourt, *Voyage d'Italie 1773-1774 avec les Dessins de Fragonard*, with introduction and notes by J. Wilhelm (Paris: Editions Michel de Romilly, 1948) 104-5. Catalogue entry by E. Einberg, 'Pierre-Jacques Volaire: Eruption of Vesuvius by Moonlight 1774', in *Grand Tour*, ed. Wilton & Bignamini (1996) 145 no. 98. Compare his dramatic painting of the 1779 eruption: *Civiltà del '700 a Napoli* (1979) 344 no. 186.

56. Catalogue entry by E. Einberg, 'Joseph Wright of Derby: Vesuvius in Eruption', in *Grand Tour*, ed. Wilton & Bignamini (1996) 149 no. 102. Compare *Civiltà del '700 a Napoli* (1979) 352 nos 191-2.

57. Catalogue entry by E. Einberg, 'Jakob Philipp Hackert: Eruption of Vesuvius in 1774', in *Grand Tour*, ed. Wilton & Bignamini (1996) 148 no. 101.

58. P. Thornton & H. Dorey, *A Miscellany of Objects from Sir John Soane's Museum* (London: Laurence King, 1992) 17.

59. C. Zintzen, *Von Pompeji nach Troja. Archäologie, Literatur und Öffentlichkeit im 19 Jahrhundert* (Vienna: WUV, Universitätsverlag, Commentarii Forschungen zur Literatur- und Kulturgeschichte no. 6, 1998) 90.

60. C. Dickens, *American Notes and Pictures from Italy* (first published 1846; Oxford: Oxford University Press, The Oxford Illustrated Dickens, 1987) 418-23.

61. Acton, *The Last Bourbons* (1961) 143.

62. W.F. Jashemski, *The Gardens of Pompeii, Herculaneum and the Villas Destroyed by Vesuvius* II (New Rochelle, NY: Caratzas brothers, 1993) 123.

63. G. Fiorelli, *Pompeianarum Antiquitatum Historia* I (Naples, 1860) part 1, 229-31, 7 Apr. 1769. At 230: 'L'Imperatore allora richiese al La Vega quanti operaj fossero impiegati in quel lavoro, ed avendo inteso che erano 30 disse al Re, come permetteva che andasse un'opera tale così languendo.'

64. Catalogue entry by A. Wilton, 'Henry Tresham: Grand Tourists purchasing antiquities', in *Grand Tour*, ed. Wilton & Bignamini (1996) 218 no. 165.

65. B. Schweitzer, *Antiken in ostpreußischem Privatbesitz* (Halle: Max Niemeyer Verlag, 1929) 197 no XXI: with Tafel XXVI.

66. W.F. Jashemski, *The Gardens of Pompeii, Herculaneum and the Villas Destroyed by Vesuvius* II (New Rochelle, NY: Caratzas brothers, 1993) 211.

67. *Voyage en Italie de M. l'Abbé Barthélemy* (Paris: F. Buisson, 1802) 33: Letter 5, 5 Nov. 1755; 41: Letter 6, 11 Nov. 1755; 100-3: Letter 16 (from M. de la Condamine), 17 Feb. 1756; 320-5: their authenticity; 322: the King of Naples.

68. J.W. von Goethe, *Italian Journey* (trans. R.R. Heitner, 1989) 261: 27 May 1787.

69. Catalogue entry by E. Einberg, 'Johann Heinrich Wilhelm Tischbein: Anna Amalia von Weimar', in *Grand Tour*, ed. Wilton & Bignamini (1996) 76 no. 34; also in *Civiltà del '700 a Napoli* (1979) 322 no. 177, where the negative point is made that even Anna Amalia was only allowed to include a monument found long ago, rather than a more recent find. Maria Carolina and artists: Acton, *The Bourbons of Naples* (1957) 214.

70. Hackert's style: Acton, *The Bourbons of Naples* (1957) 215; his privileged position at court: J.W. von Goethe, *Italian Journey* (trans. R.R. Heitner, 1989) 153: 28 Feb. 1787 and 168-9, 15 March 1787; his paintings and etchings of Pompeii: catalogue entries by I. Bignamini 'Jakob Philipp Hackert: The Ruins of Pompeii', 'View of the Theatre, Pompeii', 'View of the Interior of the Temple of Isis, Pompeii', in *Grand Tour*, ed. Wilton & Bignamini (1996) 231-2 nos 179-81, with comments on Ferdinand's motivations at 231.

71. Sir John Soane, *The Royal Academy Lectures*, ed. with introduction by D. Watkin (Cambridge: Cambridge University Press, 2000) 77, with note ad loc.

72. *Civiltà del '700 a Napoli* (1979) 418 no. 242.

73. This statue can be seen in the garden of the Museo Nazionale Giunigi at Lucca. The Latin inscription beneath it states that Maria Aloisia is '*avitae gloriae memor et custos*'.

5. The Politics of Archaeology

1. In this letter, Dumas suggests to Garibaldi the text of a decree he should issue concerning the antiquities: Dumas, *The Garibaldians in Sicily*, ch. 20, trans. Routledge (1861) 154.

2. Acton, *The Bourbons of Naples* (1957) 286-8, 463-4; *Da Palazzo degli Studi a Museo Archeologico* (Naples: Soprintendenza archeologica di Napoli 1977) 139.

3. G. Fiorelli, *Pompeianarum Antiquitatum Historia* I (Naples, 1860) part 2, 77: 2 March 1806; A. Laidlaw, 'Excavations in the Casa di Sallustio, Pompeii: a preliminary assessment', in *Eius Virtutis Studiosi: Classical and Postclassical Studies in Memory of Frank Edward Brown (1908-1988)*, ed R.T. Scott & A. Reynolds Scott (Hanover & London: National Gallery of Art, Washington & University Press of New England, Studies in the History of Art no. 43, 1993) 216-33, at 217.

4. L.A. Scatozza Höricht, 'Francesco Maria Avellino', in *La cultura classica a Napoli nell'ottocento* II (1987) 825-45, at 834.

5. A. Lancellotti, *Murat, Re di Napoli* (Florence: Casa editrice 'Nemi', 1935) 43-8.

6. Acton, *The Bourbons of Naples* (1957) 565, 634-7.

7. Acton, *The Last Bourbons* (1961) 1.

8. Acton, *The Last Bourbons* (1961) 3, 22.

9. Queen Adelaide: H.B. Van der Poel, *Corpus Topographicum Pompeianum* II. *Toponymy* (Rome: University of Texas at Austin, 1983) xix; Acton, *The Last Bourbons* (1961) 137.

10. Acton, *The Last Bourbons* (1961) 140, 145; L. Withey, *Grand Tours and Cook's Tours. A History of Leisure Travel, 1750 to 1915* (London: Aurum Press, 1998) 64-5.

11. Acton, *The Last Bourbons* (1961) 160, 170, 175.

12. Fiorelli's early career: S. De Caro, 'Giuseppe Fiorelli e gli scavi di Pompei'

139

(1999) 5-6; A. Milanese, 'L'attività giovanile di Giuseppe Fiorelli (1999) 71; de Angelis, 'Giuseppe Fiorelli' (1993) 6-7.

13. Acton, *The Last Bourbons* (1961) 161-2.

14. G. Fiorelli, *Sulle imputazioni addebitate a Giuseppe Fiorelli Ispettore degli Scavi di Pompei (arrestato a' 24 aprile 1849)* (Naples, 1849) 2, cited by de Angelis, 'Giuseppe Fiorelli' (1993) 6.

15. G. De Petra, 'Necrologie – Giuseppe Fiorelli', *Rivista italiana di numismatica* 9.1 (1896) 113-17. For the Count's letter to the King, see Dumas, *The Garibaldians in Sicily*, chap. 18, trans. Routledge (1861) 137-8.

16. De Caro, 'Giuseppe Fiorelli e gli scavi di Pompei' (1999) 5-6. Avellino's problems: Milanese, 'L'attività giovanile di Giuseppe Fiorelli' (1999) 77-82; L.A. Scatozza Höricht, 'Francesco Maria Avellino', in *La cultura classica a Napoli nell'ottocento* II (1987) 825-45, at 844-5.

17. De Caro, 'Giuseppe Fiorelli e gli scavi di Pompei' (1999) 11.

18. Milanese , 'L'attività giovanile di Giuseppe Fiorelli' (1999) 71-2, 74.

19. Acton, *The Last Bourbons* (1961) 203-5, 212-14, 223.

20. Milanese, 'L'attività giovanile di Giuseppe Fiorelli' (1999) 75.

21. This letter is cited by De Caro, 'Giuseppe Fiorelli e gli scavi di Pompei' (1999) 9-10.

22. Acton, *The Last Bourbons* (1961) 232-45.

23. Milanese, 'L'attività giovanile di Giuseppe Fiorelli' (1999) 75, 85.

24. For the regulations proposed by the 'Legge organica del Real Museo e degli Scavi di antichità', see De Caro, 'Giuseppe Fiorelli e gli scavi di Pompei' (1999) 11-15, 17-19; Milanese, 'L'attività giovanile di Giuseppe Fiorelli' (1999) 86-90.

25. Milanese, 'L'attività giovanile di Giuseppe Fiorelli' (1999) 86 cites article 1 on access and ownership.

26. De Caro, 'Giuseppe Fiorelli e gli scavi di Pompei' (1999) 20.

27. Milanese, 'L'attività giovanile di Giuseppe Fiorelli' (1999) 90-1.

28. G.M. Rispoli, 'Bernardo Quaranta', in *La cultura classica a Napoli nell'ottocento* II (1987) 505-28, at 512.

29. Milanese, 'L'attività giovanile di Giuseppe Fiorelli' (1999) 73, 91-2; De Caro, 'Giuseppe Fiorelli e gli scavi di Pompei' (1999) 20.

30. De Angelis, 'Giuseppe Fiorelli' (1993) 6-7.

31. Scatozza Höricht, 'Giuseppe Fiorelli' (1987) 869.

32. F.W. Ritschl, *Priscae Latinitatis Monumenta Epigraphica: ad archetyporum fidem exemplis lithographis repraesentata = Corpus Inscriptionum Latinarum* I, *tabulae lithographae* (Berlin: G. Riemerum, 1862).

33. Printed privately for the Count of Syracuse, then reprinted in the *Bullettino archeologico napolitano* n.s.7 (1858-59) 11-13; De Angelis, 'Giuseppe Fiorelli' (1993) 7.

34. H.B. Van der Poel, *Corpus Topographicum Pompeianum* II. *Toponymy* (Rome: University of Texas at Austin, 1983) xix: on names in general; 260-1 on 'House of the Faun'.

35. In fact, the existing Museum Director, principe di San Giorgio Spinelli, also retained his post from 1852 until his death in 1863.

36. Dumas, *The Garibaldians in Sicily*, ch. 11, trans. Routledge (1861) 91.

37. Dumas, *The Garibaldians in Sicily*, ch. 11, trans. Routledge (1861) 91-2; Collet, *Alexandre Dumas et Naples* (1994) 49, 74, 78-9.

38. Dumas, *The Garibaldians in Sicily*, ch. 1, trans. Routledge (1861) 11-12; Collet, *Alexandre Dumas et Naples* (1994) 18.

39. Dumas, *The Garibaldians in Sicily*, ch. 14, 106; ch. 15, 110, trans. Routledge (1861).

40. Dumas, *The Garibaldians in Sicily*, ch. 20, trans. Routledge (1861) 154.

41. Collet, *Alexandre Dumas et Naples* (1994) 150-3.

42. Dumas, *Le Corricolo* chs 36-41.

43. Collet, *Alexandre Dumas et Naples* (1994) 148-9.

44. Acton, *The Last Bourbons* (1961) 464-5, 497-9; Collet, *Alexandre Dumas et Naples* (1994) 153-4.

45. Collet, *Alexandre Dumas et Naples* (1994) 154-69.

46. S. Adamo Muscettola, 'Giuseppe Fiorelli e la nuova università', in *A Giuseppe Fiorelli* (1999) 145-71, at 145-6.

47. De Caro, 'Giuseppe Fiorelli e gli scavi di Pompei' (1999) 19.

48. F. Pirson, 'Giuseppe Fiorelli e gli studiosi tedeschi', in *A Giuseppe Fiorelli* (1999) 25-41, at 26, 34.

49. F. Niccolini, 'Regolamento temporaneo', in *Giornale degli scavi di Pompei* fasc. 2, ed. G. Fiorelli (Naples: 1861) 73-80.

50. L.A. Scatozza Höricht, 'Giulio Minervini', in *La cultura classica a Napoli nell'ottocento* II (1987) 847-63, at 850.

51. G. Fiorelli, *Descrizione di Pompei* (Naples: Tipografia italiana, 1875) 17; de Angelis, 'Giuseppe Fiorelli' (1993) 9.

52. De Caro, 'Giuseppe Fiorelli e gli scavi di Pompei' (1999) 20; Scatozza Höricht, 'Giuseppe Fiorelli' (1987) 873. The 'plastico': A. De Franciscis, *Guida del Museo Archeologico Nazionale di Napoli* (Cava dei Tirreni: Di Mauro editore, 1963) 101; S. De Caro, *The National Archaeological Museum of Naples* (Naples: Electa Napoli, 1996) 105.

53. Scatozza Höricht, 'Giuseppe Fiorelli' (1987) 872-3.

54. De Caro, 'Giuseppe Fiorelli e gli scavi di Pompei' (1999) 15.

55. De Caro, 'Giuseppe Fiorelli e gli scavi di Pompei' (1999) 19.

56. As pointed out by F. Delpino during discussion: 'Discussione in margine alla prima giornata', in *A Giuseppe Fiorelli* (1999) 51-67, at 66. Much more could be said about Fiorelli's reforms in the Museum, such as his plans for cataloguing the collections, but this ch. has concentrated upon his impact upon Pompeii itself.

57. F. Delpino in 'Discussione in margine alla prima giornata', in *A Giuseppe Fiorelli* (1999) 51-67, at 67.

58. S. Adamo Muscettola, 'Giuseppe Fiorelli e la nuova università', in *A Giuseppe Fiorelli* (1999) 145-71, at 154.

59. L.A. Scatozza Höricht, 'Gli studi archeologici: dall'antiquaria alla storia', in *La cultura classica a Napoli nell'ottocento* II (1987) 815-23, at 822.

60. De Caro, 'Giuseppe Fiorelli e gli scavi di Pompei' (1999) 7, 21.

61. Davis, 'Italy 1796-1870' (1997) 191.

62. L. Withey, *Grand Tours and Cook's Tours. A History of Leisure Travel, 1750 to 1915* (London: Aurum Press, 1998) 153-5.

63. C. Gasparri, 'Fiorelli e i documenti inediti per servire alla storia dei Musei d'Italia', in *A Giuseppe Fiorelli* (1999) 135-43, at 136.

64. Scatozza Höricht, 'Giuseppe Fiorelli' (1987) 872, 875.

65. C. Gasparri, 'Fiorelli e i documenti inediti per servire alla storia dei Musei d'Italia', in *A Giuseppe Fiorelli* (1999) 135-43; A. Emiliani, 'Nella battaglia tra pubblico e privato: l'istituzione della Direzione Generale e Giuseppe Fiorelli', in *A Giuseppe Fiorelli* (1999) 101-34, at 120.

66. G. De Petra, 'Necrologie – Giuseppe Fiorelli', *Rivista italiana di numismatica* 9.1 (1896) 113-17, at 116.

6. Probing Beneath the Surface

1. A. Varone, 'Pompei: conservazione, plantumazione e diserbo nella storia degli scavi', in *Archeologia e botanica. Atti del convegno di studi sul contributo della botanica alla conoscenza delle aree archeologiche vesuviane, Pompei 7-9 aprile 1989*, ed. M. Mastroroberto (Rome: Soprintendenza archeologica di Pompei, Monografie 2, «L'Erma» di Bretschneider, 1990) 39-58, at 46, with photograph taken in 1907 as fig. 10. Assessment of the likelihood of a sacred grove around the Doric Temple: Jashemski, *The Gardens of Pompeii* I (1979) 155-6, II (1993) 223.

2. A. W. van Buren, 'Studies in the archaeology of the forum at Pompeii', *Memoirs of the American Academy in Rome* 2 (1918) 67-76, at 70-1; 'Further studies in Pompeian archaeology', *Memoirs of the American Academy in Rome* 5 (1925) 103-13, at 104-5.

3. Aviary in VII.vii.16: Jashemski, *The Gardens of Pompeii* I (1979) 108, 199; II (1993) 188; A. W. van Buren, 'Further Pompeian studies', *Memoirs of the American Academy at Rome* 10 (1932) 9-54, at 10-13. Dovecote in 'House of the Faun' (VI.xii.2): Grimal, *Les Jardins Romains* (1984) 290, although this may be a misinterpretation of the evidence, since Jashemski, *The Gardens of Pompeii* I (1979) 105, states that 'no dovecots have been found thus far in the excavations', but records, II (1993) 146, the discovery of 'a carbonized branch of laurel with the bones and eggs of a dove that had made its nest in the laurel tree' there.

4. N. Purcell, 'The economy of an ancient town', *Classical Review* 40 (1990) 111-16, at 113.

5. Pliny the Elder, *Natural History* 3.5.60.

6. Jashemski, *The Gardens of Pompeii* I (1979) 80-2.

7. Jashemski, *The Gardens of Pompeii* II (1993) 330-1.

8. Grimal, *Les Jardins Romains* (1984) 12.

9. Jashemski, *The Gardens of Pompeii* I (1979) 128-9, fig. 203 on 128; II (1993) 84, 330-1.

10. Jashemski, *The Gardens of Pompeii* I (1979) 87.

11. R. Ling, *Roman Painting* (Cambridge: Cambridge University Press, 1991) 152-3.

12. G. Spano, 'III. Pompei – Relazione sulle scoperte avvenute dal 1 gennaio al 30 giugno 1910', *Notizie degli scavi di antichità* (1910) 437-86, at 447.

13. V. Spinazzola, *Pompei alla luce degli scavi nuovi di via dell'abbondanza (anni 1910-1923)* II (Rome: Libreria dello stato, 1953) on what was called then the 'House of C. Arrius Crescens', especially 728, 757-9, with figs 699, 737-9.

14. Jashemski, *The Gardens of Pompeii* II (1993) 8, 91-2.

15. Jashemski, *The Gardens of Pompeii* I (1979) 23 provides illustrations of this process.

16. Jashemski, *The Gardens of Pompeii* II (1993) 8.

17. Jashemski, *The Gardens of Pompeii* II (1993) 145-6.

18. Grimal, *Les Jardins Romains* (1984) 246. At 279 n.3, however, Grimal himself qualifies his own hypothesis, noting that new research shows that productive gardens existed alongside ornamental ones at Pompeii.

19. Jashemski, *The Gardens of Pompeii* II (1993) 153-5.

20. Jashemski, *The Gardens of Pompeii* I (1979) 19; II (1993) 127-8.

21. G. Spano, 'X. Pompei – Relazione degli scavi eseguiti nell'anno 1907', *Notizie degli scavi di antichità* (1910) 315-32, at 327.

22. Jashemski, *The Gardens of Pompeii* I (1979) 93-4; II (1993) 39-40.

23. N. Purcell, 'The Roman *villa* and the landscape of production', in *Urban Society in Roman Italy*, ed. T. J. Cornell & K. Lomas (London: University College London Press, 1995) 151-79, especially 151-61, with comments on fish as a 'cash crop' at 159.

24. Jashemski, *The Gardens of Pompeii* I (1979) 48; II (1993) 86-7: 'Estate of Julia Felix' (II.v); II (1993) 244: 'House of the Centenary' (IX.viii.6).

25. II.ix.6: Jashemski, *The Gardens of Pompeii* II (1993) 97. A more elaborate mosaic of fish in the sea, from VIII.ii.16, Mus. Naz. Nap. inv. 120177: illustrated in S. de Caro, *The National Archaeological Museum of Naples* (Naples: Electa Napoli, 1996) 142.

26. The agricultural tools: A. Maiuri, *La casa del Menandro e il suo tesoro di argenteria* I (Rome: Libreria dello stato, 1933) 461-5; J. Kolendo, 'Le attività agricole degli abitanti di Pompei e gli attrezzi agricoli ritrovati all'interno della città', *Opus* 4 (1985) 111-24. R. Ling, *The Insula of the Menander at Pompeii* I. *The structures* (Oxford: Clarendon Press, 1997) 135, 144 sounds a sceptical note, suggesting that the unusual pattern of storage evidenced by the tools implies that they may have been stored here only temporarily, and noting that several of the tools found appear more appropriate to woodworking than farming. The garden in the house: Jashemski, *The Gardens of Pompeii* II (1993) 47-9; Ling, *The Insula of the Menander* I (1997) 93.

27. Grimal, *Les Jardins Romains* (1984) 440.

28. I.ii.15: Jashemski, *The Gardens of Pompeii* II (1993) 22; I.vii.2-3: Jashemski, *The Gardens of Pompeii* II (1993) 37.

29. Jashemski, *The Gardens of Pompeii* II (1993) 59-60.

30. R.I. Curtis, 'The garum shop of Pompeii', *Cronache pompeiane* 5 (1979) 5-23; Jashemski, *The Gardens of Pompeii* II (1993) 54-5, 326.

31. Jashemski, *The Gardens of Pompeii* I (1979) ch. 3, especially 56-68; R. Ling, *Roman Painting* (Cambridge: Cambridge University Press, 1991) 152.

32. Grimal, *Les Jardins Romains* (1984) 212.

33. Jashemski, *The Gardens of Pompeii* II (1993) 341 fig. 396.

34. Jashemski, *The Gardens of Pompeii* I (1979) ch. 10; II (1993) 89-90.

35. Jashemski, *The Gardens of Pompeii* I (1979) 226-7.

36. Grimal, *Les Jardins Romains* (1984) 58: 'un morceau de campagne qui est inclu ainsi dans un jardin destiné au plaisir'.

37. Jashemski, *The Gardens of Pompeii* II (1993) 89-90.

38. Jashemski, *The Gardens of Pompeii* II (1993) 73.

39. Inn of Euxinus: Jashemski, *The Gardens of Pompeii* I (1979) 172-6; II (1993) 51-2. *Amphora* label, first published by W. F. Jashemski, 'The caupona of Euxinus at Pompeii', *Archaeology* 20 (1967) 36-44, at 37.

40. Jashemski, *The Gardens of Pompeii* II (1993) 67.

41. J. Kolendo, 'Le attività agricole degli abitanti di Pompei e gli attrezzi agricoli ritrovati all'interno della città', *Opus* 4 (1985) 111-24, at 115. Threshing floor, III.vii: Jashemski, *The Gardens of Pompeii* II (1993) 105, who suggests that it was used for beans.

42. Jashemski, *The Gardens of Pompeii* I (1979) 94-7; II (1993) 59.

43. Jashemski, *The Gardens of Pompeii* I (1979) ch. 12; II (1993) 61-3.

44. Jashemski, *The Gardens of Pompeii* I (1979) 243-6, 287, ch. 15; II (1993) 69-70.

45. Jashemski, *The Gardens of Pompeii* II (1993) 288-91: Boscoreale, 'Villa Regina'; 253, no. 522 and I (1979) 157-8: Sanctuary of Dionysus.

46. Grimal, *Les Jardins Romains* (1984) 10.

47. On the 'consumer city' model, see D.J. Mattingly, 'Beyond belief? Drawing a line beneath the consumer city', in *Roman Urbanism Beyond the Consumer City*, ed. H.M. Parkins (London & NY: Routledge, 1997) 210-18.

48. D. Nicholas, *The Growth of the Medieval City: from Late Antiquity to the Early Fourteenth Century* (London & NY: Longman, 1997) 3.

49. W. Jongman, *The Economy and Society of Pompeii* (Amsterdam: J.C. Gieben, 1988) at 133; with comments in review by N. Purcell, 'The economy of an ancient town', *Classical Review* 40 (1990) 111-16.

50. R.A. Raper, 'The analysis of the urban structure of Pompeii: a sociological examination of land use (semi-micro)', in *Spatial Archaeology*, ed. D. L. Clarke (London: Academic Press, 1977) 189-221, especially at 200.

51. *Corpus Inscriptionum Latinarum* X 874: '*salve lucru*'. Compare X 875, '*lucrum gaudium*'. The mosaics advertising *garum*: R.I. Curtis, 'A personalized floor mosaic from Pompeii', *American Journal of Archaeology* 88 (1984) 557-66.

52. Delano Smith, *Western Mediterranean Europe* (1977) ch. 4.

53. P. Horden & N. Purcell, *The Corrupting Sea. A Study of Mediterranean History* (Oxford: Blackwell, 2000) 110.

54. A. Wallace-Hadrill, 'Elites and trade in the Roman town', in *City and Country in the Ancient World*, ed. J. Rich & A. Wallace-Hadrill (London: Routledge, 1991) 241-72, especially 251 for a critique of the economic state of Pompeii at this time.

55. C. Wickham, *Early Medieval Italy. Central Power and Local Society 400-1000* (London & Basingstoke: Macmillan, 1981) 82 for the 'ruralization' of cities.

56. Delano Smith, *Western Mediterranean Europe* (1977) 131.

57. F. Braudel, *Civilization and Capitalism 15th-18th Century. I. The Structures of Everyday Life. The Limits of the Possible* (translated by S. Reynolds: Fontana Press, London 1985) 493-5.

58. Laurence, *Roman Pompeii* (1994) 67.

7. Probing Ever Deeper

1. G. De Petra, 'Necrologie – Giuseppe Fiorelli', *Rivista italiana di numismatica* 9.1 (1896) 113-17, at 116.

2. For a recent survey and critique of this approach, see Fulford & Wallace-Hadrill, 'Unpeeling Pompeii' (1998) 128, and 'Towards a history of pre-Roman Pompeii' (1999) 37-8.

3. R.C. Carrington, 'Notes on the building materials of Pompeii' *Journal of Roman Studies* 23 (1933) 125-38.

4. P. Zanker, *Pompeji. Stadtbilder als Spiegel von Gesellschaft und Herrschaftsform* (Mainz, Trierer Winckelmannsprogramme 9: 1987) 5.

5. Lepore, 'Il quadro storico' (1984) at 13-14.

6. K. Clarke, *Between Geography and History. Hellenistic Constructions of the Roman World* (Oxford: Clarendon Press, 1999) 269.

7. On the problems associated with too readily accepting invasion as an explanation for archaeological change, see E. Dench, *From Barbarians to New Men. Greek, Roman, and Modern Perceptions of Peoples from the Central Apennines* (Oxford: Clarendon Press, 1995) 186-93.

8. Nappo, 'Urban transformation at Pompeii' (1997) 91.

9. P. Zanker, *Pompeji. Stadtbilder als Spiegel von Gesellschaft und Herrschaftsform* (Mainz, Trierer Winckelmannsprogramme 9: 1987) 13; A. D'Ambrosio, 'Notiziario ufficio scavi di Pompei', *Rivista di studi pompeiani* 9 (1998) 195-6, at 196.

10. S. De Caro, review of L. Richardson, jr, *Pompeii: an architectural history* (1988) in *Gnomon* 62 (1990) 152-61, at 159.

11. Boëthius, 'Gli Etruschi in Pompei' (1932); Carrington 'The Etruscans and Pompeii' (1932) 8.

12. Boëthius, 'Gli Etruschi in Pompei' (1932) at 9-12.

13. De Caro, 'Nuove indagini sulle fortificazioni' (1985) 75-7.

14. Chiaramonte Treré, *Nuovi contributi sulle fortificazioni pompeiane* (1986) 15, 18; De Caro, 'Nuove indagini sulle fortificazioni' (1985) 79-80; in his review of L. Richardson, jr, *Pompeii: an architectural history* (1988) in *Gnomon* 62 (1990) 152-3, S. De Caro reiterates his findings on the 'pappamonte' wall in order to criticize Richardson's scepticism about its existence.

15. Chiaramonte Treré, *Nuovi contributi sulle fortificazioni pompeiane* (1986) 48; De Caro, 'Nuove indagini sulle fortificazioni' (1985) 105-6.

16. Chiaramonte Treré, *Nuovi contributi sulle fortificazioni pompeiane* (1986) 44-5.

17. De Caro, 'Nuove indagini sulle fortificazioni' (1985) 88-90.

18. For a discussion of this problem, see especially Frederiksen, 'The Etruscans in Campania' (1979).

19. Lepore, 'Il quadro storico' (1984) 16.

20. Frederiksen, 'The Etruscans in Campania' (1979) at 303.

21. Carrington 'The Etruscans and Pompeii' (1932) 8; S. De Caro, 'Lo sviluppo urbanistico di Pompei', in *Atti e memorie della Società Magna Grecia* ser.3.1 (1992) 67-90, at 71.

22. Cristofani, *Etruschi e altre genti* (1996) 123; S. De Caro, review of L.

Richardson, jr, *Pompeii: an architectural history* (1988) in *Gnomon* 62 (1990) 152-61, at 155; S. De Caro, 'Lo sviluppo urbanistico di Pompei', in *Atti e memorie della Società Magna Grecia* ser.3.1 (1992) 67-90, at 71.

23. Carrington 'The Etruscans and Pompeii' (1932) 16.

24. Cristofani, *Etruschi e altre genti* (1996) 122. The Etruscan inscriptions from Pompeii have been recently published in *Corpus Inscriptionum Etruscarum* II.2, ed. M. Cristofani, M. Pandolfini Angeletti, I. Coppola (Rome, 1996) 59-64, nos 8747-75, to which should be added the recent find in I.ix.11 published in Fulford & Wallace-Hadrill, 'Towards a history of pre-Roman Pompeii' (1999) 82-4 and 111-12.

25. Maiuri, *Alla ricerca di Pompei preromana* (1973), ch. 7, 'Greci ed Etruschi a Pompei (first published in 1954); S. De Caro, *Saggi nell'area del tempio di Apollo a Pompei. Scavi stratigrafici di A. Maiuri nel 1931-32 e 1942-43* (Naples: AION ArchStAnt Quad. no. 3, 1986) especially 20-4; De Caro, 'Nuove indagini sulle fortificazioni' (1985) 112.

26. Necropolis: *Corpus Inscriptionum Etruscarum* II.2, ed. M. Cristofani, M. Pandolfini Angeletti, I. Coppola (Rome, 1996) nos 8774-5; S. De Caro, 'Lo sviluppo urbanistico di Pompei', in *Atti e memorie della Società Magna Grecia* ser. 3.1 (1992) 67-90, at 74. Frederiksen, 'The Etruscans in Campania' (1979) hypothesized a period of influence from the sixth to late fifth centuries BC.

27. Frederiksen, 'The Etruscans in Campania' (1979) 281; Cristofani, *Etruschi e altre genti* (1996) 123; E. La Rocca, M. & A. de Vos, *Pompei* (Milan: Guide archeologiche Mondadori, 1994) 12.

28. De Caro, 'La città sannitica urbanistica e architettura' (1991) at 24.

29. The 'Altstadt' tradition is reviewed by J.B. Ward-Perkins, 'Note di topografia e urbanistica', in *Pompei 79*, ed. F. Zevi (Naples: Gaetano Macchiaroli editore, 1984) 25-39, at 29.

30. F. Haverfield, *Ancient Town Planning* (Oxford: Clarendon Press, 1913) 65-7 argued strongly for the 'Altstadt' theory, but see R. Laurence, *Roman Pompeii. Space and Society* (London & NY: Routledge, 1994) 12-16 and 'Modern ideology and the creation of ancient town planning', *European Review of History* 1 (1994) 9-18 for the impact of Haverfield's intellectual context within the town-planning debate of early twentieth-century Britain upon this theory.

31. H. Geertman, 'The layout of the city and its history. The Dutch project', in *Unpeeling Pompeii* (1998) 17-25.

32. D'Ambrosio & De Caro, 'Un contributo all'architettura e all'urbanistica' (1989) 194-7; De Caro, 'La città sannitica urbanistica e architettura' (1991) 25.

33. D'Ambrosio & De Caro, 'Un contributo all'architettura e all'urbanistica' (1989).

34. Bonghi Jovino, *Ricerche a Pompei* (1984), especially M. Bonghi Jovino, 'Osservazioni conclusive' 357-71 and L. Castelletti, 'Analisi dei legni' 352-5.

35. Fulford & Wallace-Hadrill, 'Towards a history of pre-Roman Pompeii' (1999) 98-101, quoting 101.

36. Fulford & Wallace-Hadrill, 'Towards a history of pre-Roman Pompeii' (1999) 106-7.

37. Cristofani, 'La fase 'etrusca' di Pompei' (1991) 16-17, with comments of Fulford & Wallace-Hadrill, 'Towards a history of pre-Roman Pompeii' (1999) 105.

38. S. De Caro, review of L. Richardson, jr, *Pompeii: an architectural history*

(1988) in *Gnomon* 62 (1990) 152-61, at 155 and Maiuri, *Alla ricerca di Pompei preromana* (1973), ch. 8 'Saggi nella 'Casa della Fontana Grande' e in altre case pompeiane' (first published in 1944-5).

39. Fulford & Wallace-Hadrill, 'Unpeeling Pompeii' (1998) 131.

40. Fulford & Wallace-Hadrill, 'Towards a history of pre-Roman Pompeii' (1999) 50, 103, 109.

41. Fulford & Wallace-Hadrill, 'Towards a history of pre-Roman Pompeii' (1999) 103.

42. Fulford & Wallace-Hadrill, 'Towards a history of pre-Roman Pompeii' (1999) 105.

43. Fulford & Wallace-Hadrill, 'The House of Amarantus at Pompeii' (1995-6) 98.

44. Bonghi Jovino, *Ricerche a Pompei* (1984) 39, 385.

45. Nappo, 'Urban transformation at Pompeii' (1997) 91.

46. A. D'Ambrosio, 'Notiziario ufficio scavi di Pompei', *Rivista di studi pompeiani* 9 (1998) 195-6, at 196; P.G. Guzzo, 'Alla ricerca della Pompei sannitica', in *Studi sull'Italia dei Sanniti* (Milan: Soprintendenza archeologica di Roma, Electa, 2000) 107-17, at 109.

47. Maiuri, *Alla ricerca di Pompei preromana* (1973) 116-18; De Caro, 'La città sannitica urbanistica e architettura' (1991) at 32.

48. Arthur, 'Problems of the urbanization of Pompeii' (1986) 33; De Caro, 'La città sannitica urbanistica e architettura' (1991) at 32.

49. Maiuri, *Alla ricerca di Pompei preromana* (1973) 86-7.

50. De Caro, 'La città sannitica urbanistica e architettura' (1991) 32.

51. Arthur, 'Problems of the urbanization of Pompeii' (1986) 35.

52. De Caro, 'La città sannitica urbanistica e architettura' (1991) 30.

53. The Oscan monumental inscriptions from Pompeii are published in E. Vetter, *Handbuch der italischen Dialekte* (Heidelberg: C. Winter, 1953) nos 8-22, updated by R. Antonini, 'Iscrizioni osche pompeiane', *Studi etruschi* 45 (1977) 317-40, part of A.L. Prosdocimi, 'Rivista di epigrafia italica', 317-47 and by P. Poccetti, *Nuovi documenti italici: a complemento del Manuale di E. Vetter* (Pisa: Giardini, Orientamenti linguistici 8, 1979) nos 107-10.

54. Maiuri, 'Pompeii: Santuario Dionisiaco in località S. Abbondio' (1947); Van Buren, 'Archaeological news: Italy: Pompeii' (1948) 509; Pugliese Carratelli, *Tra Cadmo e Orfeo* (1990) 431; Elia & Pugliese Carratelli, 'Il santuario dionisiaco' (1979) 449-50; Jashemski, *The Gardens of Pompeii* I (1979) 158.

55. P. Poccetti, *Nuovi documenti italici: a complemento del Manuale di E. Vetter* (Pisa: Giardini, Orientamenti linguistici 8, 1979) nos 107-8; Elia & Pugliese Carratelli, 'Il santuario dionisiaco' (1979) 448-9.

56. Maiuri, 'Pompeii: Santuario Dionisiaco in località S. Abbondio' (1947); Van Buren, 'Archaeological news: Italy: Pompeii' (1948) 509; Elia & Pugliese Carratelli, 'Il santuario dionisiaco' (1979) 458-69.

57. Pugliese Carratelli, *Tra Cadmo e Orfeo* (1990) 431-2.

58. P. Zanker, *Pompeji. Stadtbilder als Spiegel von Gesellschaft und Herrschaftsform* (Mainz, Trierer Winckelmannsprogramme 9: 1987) ch. 1.

59. On the role of architecture in controlling the visitor's experience of this house, see M. Grahame, 'Public and private in the Roman house: the spatial order of the Casa del Fauno', in *Domestic Space in the Roman World: Pompeii and Beyond*, ed. R. Laurence & A. Wallace-Hadrill (Portsmouth, RI: *Journal of Roman Archaeology* supplement 22, 1997) 137-64.

60. P. Zanker, *Pompeji. Stadtbilder als Spiegel von Gesellschaft und Herrschaftsform* (Mainz, Trierer Winckelmannsprogramme 9: 1987) 6-9; F. Zevi, 'La città sannitica. L'edilizia privata e la Casa del Fauno' in *Pompei* I, ed. F. Zevi (Naples: Banco di Napoli, 1991) 47-74, especially at 70-1; S.C. Nappo, *Pompeii. Guide to the Lost City* (London: Weidenfeld & Nicolson, 1998) 136-40; A. & M. de Vos, *Pompei, Ercolano, Stabia* (Rome & Bari: Guide archeologiche Laterza, 1988) 160-4.

Further Reading

1. Prologue to the Nightmare

Discussion of the disputed date of the major earthquake in Nero's reign can be found in G.O. Onorato, 'La data del terremoto di Pompei, 5 febbraio 62 d.Cr.', *Rendiconti dell'Accademia Nazionale dei Lincei. Classe di scienze morali, storiche e filologiche* ser. 8, vol. 4, fasc. 11-12 (1949) 644-61, presenting arguments in favour of dating the earthquake to 62, not 63 and, more recently, H. Hine, 'The date of the Campanian earthquake. AD 62 or AD 63, or both?', *L'Antiquité Classique* 53 (1984) 266-69, assessing possible reasons for the discrepancy in dating 'the earthquake' between Tacitus and Seneca.

Analysis of the archaeological evidence for structural damage caused by earthquakes is provided by J-P. Adam, 'Observations techniques sur les suites du séisme de 62 à Pompéi', in *Tremblements de terre, éruptions volcaniques et vie des hommes dans la Campanie antique*, ed. C.A. Livadie (Naples: Centre Jean Bérard, 1986) 67-87 = 'Osservazioni techniche sugli effetti del terremoto di Pompei del 62 d.C', in *I terremoti prima del Mille in Italia e nell'area mediterranea*, ed. E. Guidoboni (Bologna: SGA Storia-Geofisica-Ambiente, 1989) 460-74, giving a detailed survey of architectural evidence for the Pompeians' reponses to earthquake damage.

The likely social and economic impact of a major earthquake is explored by Jean Andreau in two articles: 'Histoire des séismes et histoire économique. Le tremblement de terre de Pompéi (62 ap. J.-C.)', *Annales. Économies, Sociétés, Civilisations* 28 (1973) 369-95, a comparative study of the social and economic effects of major earthquakes, and 'Il terremoto del 62', in *Pompei 79*, ed. F. Zevi (Naples: Gaetano Macchiaroli editore, 1984) 40-4, presenting an assessment of what priorities the Pompeians adopted in restoring the town following the earthquake. A number of studies have followed on from A. Maiuri, *L'ultima fase edilizia di Pompei* (Spoleto: Istituto di studi romani, 1942) in presenting a picture of Pompeian society in crisis during its last period of existence, notably several articles by Penelope Allison: 'Artefact assemblages: not "the Pompeii Premise" ', in *Papers of the Fourth Conference of Italian Archaeology* III. *New Developments in Italian Archaeology,* Part 1, eds E. Herring, R. Whitehouse, J. Wilkins (London: Accordia Research Centre, 1992) 49-56; 'On-going seismic activity and its effects on the living conditions in Pompeii in the last decades', in *Archäologie und Seismologie* (see below) 183-90; 'Roman households: an archaeological perspective', in *Roman Urbanism Beyond the Consumer City*, ed. H.M. Parkins (London & NY: Routledge, 1997) 112-46.

New work questioning the nature of seismic damage at Pompeii during its last phase can be found in the conference proceedings of a joint meeting of archaeologists and vulcanologists *Archäologie und Seismologie. La regione vesuviana dal 62 al 79 d.C. Problemi archeologici e sismologici* (Munich: Biering & Brinkmann,

1995), and R. Ling, *The Insula of the Menander at Pompeii*. I. *The Structures* (Oxford: Clarendon Press, 1997), which includes a detailed examination of structural damage in one particular *insula*.

Debate about the state of the Forum in 79 still continues. Opposing views may be found in Mau & Dobbins: A. Mau, 'Il portico del foro di Pompei', *Mittheilungen des Kaiserlich Deutschen Archaeologischen Instituts. Roemische Abteilung* 6 (1891) 168-76, and *Pompeii. Its Life and Art*, trans. F.W. Kelsey (London: Macmillan, 1899), chs 8, 14-15; J.J. Dobbins, 'Problems of chronology, decoration, and urban design in the Forum at Pompeii', *American Journal of Archaeology* 98.4 (1994) 629-94. For a balanced view, see K. Wallat, 'Der Zustand des Forums von Pompeji am Vorabend des Vesuvausbruchs 79 n. Chr.', in *Archäologie und Seismologie* (see above) 75-89. Original documentation relating to the excavations is contained in the three volumes of excavation day-books edited by G. Fiorelli, *Pompeianarum Antiquitatum Historia* (Naples, 1860, 1862, 1864).

2. The Nightmare Revealed

The following is a selection of the many articles written over the last couple of decades or so by archaeologists and vulcanologists re-assessing the overall character of the eruption in 79: S. Sparks, 'Dusts of destruction', *New Scientist* 59 (1973) 134-6; H. Sigurdsson, S. Cashdollar, S.R.J. Sparks, 'The eruption of Vesuvius in AD 79: reconstruction from historical and volcanological evidence', *American Journal of Archaeology* 86 (1982) 39-51; U. Pappalardo, 'L'eruzione pliniana del Vesuvio nel 79 d.C.: Ercolano', in *Volcanologie et Archéologie*, eds C. Albore Livadie & F. Widemann (Strasbourg: *PACT* 25, 1990) 197-215; T. Pescatore & H. Sigurdsson, 'L'eruzione del Vesuvio del 79 d.C.', in *Ercolano 1738-1988. 250 anni di ricerca archeologica*, ed. L. Franchi dell'Orto (Rome: «L'Erma» di Bretschneider, 1993) 449-58; R. Scandone, 'I meccanismi eruttivi dell'eruzione del 79 d.C. del Vesuvio', in *Archäologie und Seismologie* (1995: see above) 137-41; C. Luongo, A. Perrotta, C. Scarpati, 'The eruption of AD 79', in *Pompeii. Life in a Roman Town*, ed. A. Ciarallo & E. De Carolis (Milan: Electa, 1999) 31-3; H. Sigurdsson, *Melting the Earth. The History of Ideas on Volcanic Eruptions* (Oxford & NY: Oxford University Press, 1999), ch. 5.

This has totally transformed our picture of the processes by which Pompeii was destroyed and has prompted archaeologists to undertake new research into tracing the course of the eruption with more accuracy. Refinements are constantly being made to the picture of the sequence of volcanic deposits and activity, for example in the new excavations in the area of the 'House of the Chaste Lovers' (IX.xii.6-7): A. Varone & A. Marturano, 'L'eruzione vesuviana del 24 agosto del 79 d.C. attraverso le lettere di Plinio il Giovane e le nuove evidenze archeologiche', *Rivista di studi pompeiani* 8 (1997) 57-72. A new appreciation is emerging of the information that can be extracted from patterns like the distribution of bodies in the town: E. De Carolis, G. Patricelli, A. Ciarallo, 'Rinvenimenti di corpi umani nell'area urbana di Pompei', *Rivista di studi pompeiani* 9 (1998) 75-123.

More technical discussions of the timetable and progress of the eruption can be found in scientific journals: D.V. Kent, D. Ninkovich, T. Pescatore, S.R.J. Sparks, 'Palaeomagnetic determination of emplacement temperature of Vesuvius AD 79 pyroclastic deposits', *Nature* 290 (1981) 393-6; S. Carey & H. Sigurdsson, 'Temporal variations in column height and magma discharge rate during the 79 AD eruption of Vesuvius', *Geological Society of America. Bulletin* 99.2 (1987) 303-14; *Journal of Volcanology and Geothermal Research* 58.1-4 (1993) – *Special issue: Mount Vesuvius*, eds B. De Vivo, R. Scandone & R. Trigila, with articles by R. Scandone, L. Giacomelli, P. Gasparini, 'Mount Vesuvius: 2000 years of volcanological observations', 5-25, and P. Papale & F. Dobran, 'Modeling of the ascent of magma during the plinian eruption of Vesuvius in AD 79', 101-32.

For further scientific information on volcanic eruptions in general, see H. Sigurdsson, ed., *Encyclopedia of Volcanoes* (San Diego: Academic Press, 2000). The *National Geographic Magazine* 159.1 (January 1981) provides terrifying photographs and eye-witness accounts of the Mount St Helens eruption the previous May.

3. A Broken Sleep

The likelihood that material was salvaged from Pompeii in the immediate aftermath of the eruption as a result of private and public initiatives is assessed by J-P. Descoeudres, 'Did some Pompeians return to their city after the eruption of Mt Vesuvius in AD 79? Observations in the House of the Coloured Capitals', in *Ercolano 1738-1988. 250 anni di ricerca archeologica* ed. F. Franchi dell'Orto (Rome: «L'Erma» di Bretschneider, 1993) 165-78; F. Zevi, 'Sul Tempio di Iside a Pompei', in *La Parola del Passato: Alla ricerca di Iside* 49.1-2 (1994) 37-56, at 51-6.

Several articles discuss evidence for activity around Pompeii after 79. The earliest extensive argument in favour of the regeneration of the Vesuvian area was presented by A. Sogliano, 'La rinascita di Pompei', *Rendiconti dell'Accademia dei Lincei* ser.5, vol. 24 (1915) 483-514, whose proposal was peremptorily dismissed by A. Maiuri, 'Gli scavi di Pompei dal 1879 al 1948', in *Pompeiana. Raccolta di studi per il secondo centenario degli scavi di Pompei* (Naples: Gaetano Macchiaroli editore, 1950) 9-40, at 21, and criticised again by V. Castiglione Morelli del Franco, 'Il Giornale dei Soprastanti di Pompei e le Notizie degli Scavi' in *Ercolano 1738-1988. 250 anni di ricerca archeologica* ed. F. Franchi dell'Orto (Rome: «L'Erma» di Bretschneider, 1993) 659-66, at 663. Nevertheless, the issue has been revisited over the years, as new archaeological evidence has turned up: G. Alagi, 'La zona vesuviana dal I al IV secolo', *Campania Sacra* 2 (1971) 3-13; G. Cerulli Irelli, 'Intorno al problema della rinascita di Pompei', in *Neue Forschungen in Pompeji und den anderen vom Vesuvausbruch 79 n. Chr. verschütteten Städten*, ed. B. Andreae & H. Kyrieleis (Recklinghausen: Verlag Aurel Bongers, 1975) 291-8; M. Pagano, 'L'area vesuviana dopo l'eruzione del 79 d.C.', *Rivista di studi pompeiani* 7 (1995-6) 35-44; E. De Carolis, 'Testimonianze archeologiche in area vesuviana posteriori al 79 d.C.', *Archeologia, uomo, territorio* 16 (1997) 17-32; G. Soricelli, 'La regione vesuviana dopo l'eruzione del 79 d.C.', *Athenaeum* 85 (1997) 139-54; E. De Carolis, 'Rinvenimenti di tombe posteriori al 79 d.C. in area vesuviana', in *Pompei oltre la vita. Nuove testimonianze dalle necropoli* (Naples: Soprintendenza di Pompei, 1998) 113-17.

More recent disturbances to the site, from the late sixteenth century until 'official' excavations began, and the various interpretations made of the scattered finds are set out by G.W. Bowersock, 'The rediscovery of Herculaneum and Pompeii', *The American Scholar* 47 (1978) 461-70. The course of the aqueduct is traced by D. Russo, *Il tempio di Giove Meilichio a Pompei* (Naples: Accademia di archeologia, lettere e belle arti di Napoli, Monumenti no. 8, 1991) ch. 3. On the cultural context of Sannazaro, see C. Kidwell, *Sannazaro and Arcadia* (London: Duckworth, 1993); a text of *Arcadia* can be found edited by E. Carrara (Turin: Collezione di classici italiani no. 46, 1948). Finally, a rare contemporary description of the site in 1776, not long after the official excavations began, was only published in 1953: F. Latapie, 'Description des fouilles de Pompéii (a.1776)', with introduction by P. Barrière and notes by A. Maiuri, *Rendiconti della Accademia di archeologica, lettere e belle arti* n.s. 28 (1953) 223-48.

4. The Reawakening

The course of the Bourbon rule of Charles VII and Ferdinand IV is traced in detail by H. Acton, *The Bourbons of Naples (1734-1825)* (London: Methuen, corrected edn 1957), and more briefly in two chapters by D. Carpanetto, 'Bourbon Italy: Naples and Parma' and 'Enlightenment and reform in Naples and Sicily', in *Italy in the Age of Reason 1685-1789*, ed. D. Carpanetto & G. Ricuperati, trans. C. Higgitt (London & NY: Longman, History of Italy vol. 5, 1987) 179-92, 236-48. The main cultural features of the period are discussed by R. Oresko, 'Culture in the age of baroque and rococo', in *The Oxford Illustrated History of Italy*, ed. G. Holmes (Oxford: Oxford University Press 1997) 139-76, and illustrated in the exhibition catalogue, *Civiltà del '700 a Napoli 1734-1799* I (Florence: Centro Di, 1979). A. Allroggen-Bedel, 'Archäologie und Politik: Herculaneum und Pompeji im 18 Jahrhundert', *Hephaistos* 14 (1996) 217-52 examines the political significance of antiquities for these rulers, something which may be further illustrated by considering the history of the development of Naples Archaeological Museum: E. Pozzi Paolini, 'Il Museo Archeologico Nazionale di Napoli in due secoli di vita', in *Da Palazzo degli Studi a Museo Archeologico. Mostra storico-documentaria del Museo Nazionale di Napoli* (Naples: Soprintendenza Archeologica di Napoli, 1977) 1-27; S. De Caro, *The National Archaeological Museum of Naples* (Naples: Electa Napoli, 1996).

The role of foreigners as visitors to and viewers of the sites, museum, and volcano is illustrated by A. Wilton & I. Bignamini, *Grand Tour. The Lure of Italy in the Eighteenth Century* (London: Tate Gallery, 1996); C. Grell, *Herculanum et Pompéi dans les récits des voyageurs français du XVIIIe siècle* (Naples: Centre Jean Bérard, Mémoires et documents sur Rome et l'Italie méridionale, 1982); I. Jenkins & K. Sloan, *Vases and Volcanoes. Sir William Hamilton and his Collection* (London: British Museum, 1996). A translation of Goethe's *Italian Journey* is available in *The Collected Works*, VI, trans. R.R. Heitner, with introduction and notes by T.P. Saine, ed. T.P. Saine & J.L. Sammons (Princeton, NJ: Princeton University Press, 1989). The excavation of the Temple of Isis, and early reactions to it are fully documented in S. De Caro, ed., *Alla ricerca di Iside. Analisi, studi e restauri dell'Iseo pompeiano nel Museo di Napoli* (Rome: Soprintendenza archeologica per le province di Napoli e Caserta, Arti S.p.A., 1992).

5. The Politics of Archaeology

On the overall historical context of nineteenth-century Italy, see J.A. Davis, 'Italy 1796-1870: the Age of the Risorgimento', in *The Oxford Illustrated History of Italy*, ed. G. Holmes (Oxford: Oxford University Press, 1997) 177-209. The history of Bourbon Naples is explored in depth by H. Acton in two books: *The Bourbons of Naples (1734-1825)* (London: Methuen, corrected edn 1957) and *The Last Bourbons of Naples (1825-1861)* (London: Methuen, 1961).

For a detailed account of the career of Alexandre Dumas at Naples, see A. Collet, *Alexandre Dumas et Naples* (Geneva: Slatkine, Dimensioni del Viaggio no. 6, 1994). His account of Garibaldi's triumph has been translated as *The Garibaldians in Sicily*, trans. E. Routledge (London: Routledge, Warne & Routledge, 1861). He describes his earlier travels to Pompeii in *Impressions de Voyage. Le Corricolo* II (Plan de la Tour (Var): Editions d'Aujourd'hui, L'Imprimerie de Provence, 1978).

The career of Giuseppe Fiorelli is outlined by L.A. Scatozza Höricht, 'Giuseppe Fiorelli', in *La cultura classica a Napoli nell'ottocento* II (Naples: Pubblicazioni del Dipartimento di filologia classica dell'Università degli Studi di Napoli, 1987) 865-80 and by F. de Angelis, 'Giuseppe Fiorelli: la «vecchia» antiquaria di fronte allo scavo', in *Ricerche di Storia dell'arte* 50: *L'archeologia italiana dall'Unità al novecento*, ed. S. Settis (1993) 6-16, and re-assessed in detail by the collection of papers edited by V. Castiglione Morelli, *A Giuseppe Fiorelli nel primo centenario della morte* (Atti del convegno Napoli 19-20 marzo 1997: Naples: Arte tipografica, 1999), of which the following are particularly useful: S. De Caro, 'Giuseppe Fiorelli e gli scavi di Pompei', 5-23; A. Milanese, 'L'attività giovanile di Giuseppe Fiorelli e l'esperienza nella commissione per le riforme del Museo Borbonico: nascita di un protagonista della storia della tutela in Italia', 69-100. The overall background of archaeological studies in Naples during the nineteenth century is dealt with in an extensive section in *La cultura classica a Napoli nell'ottocento* II (Naples: Pubblicazioni del Dipartimento di filologia classica dell'Università degli Studi di Napoli, 1987).

6. Probing Beneath the Surface

The classic synthesis of Roman gardens is P. Grimal, *Les Jardins Romains* (Paris: Fayard, 1984, 3rd edn). The material that forms the basis of this chapter can be found in W.F. Jashemski, *The Gardens of Pompeii, Herculaneum and the Villas Destroyed by Vesuvius* (New Rochelle, NY: Caratzas brothers, 2 vols 1979 and 1993). Jashemski's work is set into the context of land use for production and consumption in the town as a whole by R. Laurence, *Roman Pompeii. Space and Society* (London and NY: Routledge, 1994) ch. 4 'Production and consumption', especially at 64-8. For the wider historical context of agriculture within towns, see C. Delano Smith, *Western Mediterranean Europe. A historical geography of Italy, Spain and Southern France since the Neolithic* (London: Academic Press, 1979) ch. 4, 'The urban farmer'.

7. Probing Ever Deeper

The presence of Etruscans at Pompeii has been much debated: A. Boëthius, 'Gli Etruschi in Pompei', in *Symbolae Philologicae O.A. Danielsson octogenario dicatae* (Uppsala: A.-B. Lundequistska bokhandeln, 1932) 1-12; R.C. Carrington, 'The Etruscans and Pompeii', *Antiquity* 6 (1932) 5-23; M. Frederiksen, 'The Etruscans in Campania', in *Italy Before the Romans: The Iron Age, Orientalizing and Etruscan Periods*, ed. D. & F.R. Ridgway (London, NY, San Francisco: Academic Press, 1979) 277-311; E. Lepore, 'Il quadro storico', in *Pompei 79*, ed. F. Zevi (Naples: Gaetano Macchiaroli editore, 1984) 13-23; M. Cristofani, 'La fase "etrusca" di Pompei', in *Pompei* I, ed. F. Zevi (Naples: Banco di Napoli, 1991) 9-22 and *Etruschi e altre genti nell'Italia preromana. Mobilità in età arcaica* (Rome: Archaeologica 120, Bretschneider, 1996) 111-25.

Stratigraphic excavations (listed here in chronological order) have now revealed a much more complicated picture of archaic Pompeii: A. Maiuri, *Alla ricerca di Pompei preromana* (Naples: Società editrice Napoletana, 1973); M. Bonghi Jovino, ed., *Ricerche a Pompei. L'insula 5 della Regio VI dalle origini al 79 d.C.* (Rome: «L'Erma» di Bretschneider, 1984); S. De Caro, 'Nuove indagini sulle fortificazioni di Pompei', *A.I.O.N. Archeologia e storia antica* 7 (1985) 75-114; C. Chiaramonte Treré, *Nuovi contributi sulle fortificazioni pompeiane* (Milan: Quaderni di Acme 6, Università degli studi di Milano, Facoltà di lettere e filosofia, 1986); P. Arthur, 'Problems of the urbanization of Pompeii: excavations 1980-1981', *The Antiquaries Journal* 66 (1986) 29-44; A. D'Ambrosio & S. De Caro, 'Un contributo all'architettura e all'urbanistica di Pompei in età ellenistica. I saggi nella casa VII, 4, 62', *A.I.O.N. Archeologia e storia antica* 11 (1989) 173-215; S. De Caro, 'La città sannitica urbanistica e architettura', in *Pompei* I, ed. F. Zevi (Naples: Banco di Napoli, 1991) 23-46 and 'Lo sviluppo urbanistico di Pompei', in *Atti e memorie della Società Magna Grecia* ser. 3.1 (1992) 67-90; S.C. Nappo, 'Urban transformation at Pompeii in the late 3rd and early 2nd century BC', in *Domestic Space in the Roman World: Pompeii and Beyond*, ed. R. Laurence & A. Wallace-Hadrill (Portsmouth RI: JRA supplement no. 22, 1997) 91-120; M. Fulford & A. Wallace-Hadrill, 'The House of Amarantus at Pompeii (I,9,11-12): an interim report on survey and excavations in 1995-96', *Rivista di studi pompeiani* 77-113, 'Unpeeling Pompeii', *Antiquity* 72 (1998) 128-45, and 'Towards a history of pre-Roman Pompeii: excavations beneath the House of Amarantus (I.9.11-12), 1995-98', *Papers of the British School at Rome* 67 (1999) 37-144; J. Berry, ed., *Unpeeling Pompeii. Studies in Region I of Pompeii* (Milan: Soprintendenza archeologica di Pompei, Electa, 1998).

The Sanctuary of Dionysus in 'località S. Abbondio' has not been published in full, but the essentials can be found in A. Maiuri, 'Pompeii: Santuario Dionisiaco in località S. Abbondio', *Fasti archaeologici* 2 (1947) 197 no. 1656; A.W. Van Buren, 'Archaeological news: Italy: Pompeii', *American Journal of Archaeology* 52 (1948) 508-9; W.F. Jashemski, *The Gardens of Pompeii, Herculaneum and the Villas Destroyed by Vesuvius* (New Rochelle, NY: Caratzas brothers, 1979 and 1993) I, 157-8 and II 253, no. 522; O. Elia & G. Pugliese Carratelli, 'Il santuario dionisiaco di Pompei', *Parola del Passato* 34 (1979) 442-81; G. Pugliese Carratelli, *Tra Cadmo e Orfeo. Contributi alla storia civile e religiosa dei Greci d'Occidente* (Bologna: Società editrice il Mulino, 1990) 431-9.

Glossary

aedile: local magistrate in charge of public buildings.

'Altstadt': area thought to form nucleus of original settlement.

amphora/-ae: pottery transport container, often used for olive oil and wine.

ashlar masonry: building technique, using squared blocks of stone.

atrium: main reception room of a house, with *impluvium* in the middle, leading to other rooms.

'bucchero' pottery: black terracotta ware, widespread from the mid-seventh to fifth century BC.

caldera: large hollow in a volcano.

'cappucina' burials: simple form of burial, using tiles as a covering.

cella: innermost part of a temple, where deity's statue was housed.

decurion: local town councillor.

forum: open piazza in a town, surrounded by public buildings; the focus of religious, commercial, administrative, and judicial affairs.

fullery: laundry where clothes were cleaned and finished.

garum: fish sauce.

impluvium: square pool in the middle of the *atrium*'s floor, for collecting rainwater from roof.

insula: block of buildings defined by streets on all sides.

lararium: shrine for the household gods.

macellum: meat and fish market-building in the *forum*.

magma: fluid or semifluid discharge from a volcano.

opus Africanum: building technique: wall framework of upright limestone blocks, filled in with rubble.

opus incertum: building technique: wall with rubble and mortar core, faced with irregularly shaped medium-sized stones.

opus signinum: water-proof flooring.

Oscan: one of the local languages of Italy, used in Campania, which was gradually replaced by Latin.

pappamonte tufa: blocks of dark grey tufa, formed from compacted volcanic ash.

peristyle: open courtyard surrounded by a portico.

phreatomagmatic explosion: volcanic explosion caused by the heating of underground water.

pisolites: pea-like rounded grains of limestone.

pumice: light, porous stone discharged from a volcano.

pyroclastic flow: hot avalanche of pumice, ash, and gases.

pyroclastic surge: cloud of volcanic ash and hot gases.

Risorgimento: movement which began in the early nineteenth century, leading to the proclamation of the Kingdom of Italy (1861), and eventually to Unification (1871).

synoecism: the process of state formation, when several neighbouring villages coalesce into a single settlement.

tablinum: room between *atrium* and peristyle, thought to be where the householder conducted his business.

triclinium: space for dining, with couches.

tufa: stone formed from compacted volcanic ash.

villa rustica: estate in the countryside.

Timeline: Events relating to the destruction, rediscovery, and excavation of Pompeii

62	A major earthquake rocks Pompeii and surrounding area.
79	Eruption of Vesuvius burying Pompeii, Herculaneum, and environs.
1504	Publication of Sannazaro's *Arcadia*.
1594	Construction begins of aqueduct between Sarno and Torre Annunziata, which cuts through the site.
1631	Violent eruption of Vesuvius.
1637	Antiquarian Lucas Holstenius correctly identifies the site of Pompeii.
1689	Inscription discovered with the letters 'POMPEI'.
1734	Charles VII accedes to the throne of the Kingdom of the Two Sicilies.
1748	Official excavations begin at Pompeii: Amphitheatre, 'Street of Tombs' and nearby houses explored.
1755	Royal Herculaneum Academy founded; nine volumes of *Le Antichità di Ercolano esposte* published between 1757 and 1796.
1759	Charles VII becomes Charles III of Spain, and Ferdinand IV takes over at Naples as a minor.
1764	Severe famine at Naples. Temple of Isis uncovered.
1806	Joseph Bonaparte becomes ruler of Naples.
1808-15	Joachim Murat takes over as ruler of Naples.
1813-16	Amphitheatre re-excavated and cleared. Forum excavated from 1814.
1815	Bourbon restoration: return of Ferdinand IV, who becomes Ferdinand I a year later.
1830-32	'House of the Faun' excavated.
1844	Visit of Charles Dickens. Start of political unrest in Naples.
1848	'Commission for the Reorganization and Reform of the Bourbon Museum and the ancient Excavations in the Kingdom'.
1860	Expulsion of the Bourbon monarchy and annexation of Naples to the Kingdom of Italy.
1864	First Italian tours of Thomas Cook.
1866	School of Archaeology at Pompeii established by Fiorelli.
1894-95	'House of the Vettii' excavated.
1902	Eruption of Mount Pelée, Martinique.
1943	Parts of Pompeii hit by allied bombs during World War II.
1944	Most recent eruption of Vesuvius.
1980	Eruption of Mount St Helens, north-western USA.

Key figures in the history of Pompeii's excavation

Charles VII (Bourbon): Accedes to the throne of the Kingdom of the Two Sicilies in 1734, and eagerly promotes the earliest official excavations of Pompeii from 1748 to 1759. Later Charles III of Spain.

Alexandre Dumas: French novelist; supporter of Garibaldi; briefly honorary director of Naples Museum and Pompeii in 1860.

Ferdinand IV (Bourbon): Takes over from Charles VII in 1759, and is less inclined than his father to dig at Pompeii. Becomes Ferdinand I of the Two Sicilies in 1816 after his restoration following Napoleonic rule in Naples in 1815.

Giuseppe Fiorelli: Director of Pompeii from 1860 and Naples Museum from 1863 to 1875, when he became Director General of Antiquities.

Jakob Philipp Hackert: Painter favoured by Queen Maria Carolina at Naples; he produced realistic representations of Vesuvius erupting and the site at Pompeii.

Sir William Hamilton: British ambassador to Naples from 1764 to 1800, keen observer of Vesuvius' eruptions and collector of antiquities.

Wilhelmina Jashemski: Emeritus Professor, Dept. of History, University of Maryland. Systematically studied the site's gardens in the1960/70s.

Amedeo Maiuri: Director of Pompeii, 1924 to 1960. Excavated 'Villa of Mysteries', 'House of the Menander'; carried out series of stratigraphic soundings in the Forum, at the town walls, and in various private houses.

Joachim Murat: Husband of Napoleon's sister, Caroline; ruler of Naples from 1808. Together with his wife, keen promoter of the excavations, clearing the Amphitheatre and Forum.

Antonio Sogliano: Director of Pompeii, 1905-10. Excavated outside the 'Vesuvian Gate', and claimed that a second Pompeii grew up in this area following the eruption.

Giuseppe Spano: One of the first scholars to be interested in the site's natural environment in the early twentieth century.

Vittorio Spinazzola: Director of Pompeii, 1911 to 1923. Excavated lower section of the 'Street of Abundance'; first made plaster casts of tree-roots cavities.

Bernardo Tanucci: Regency minister for Ferdinand IV, founder of the Royal Herculaneum Academy.

J. J. Winckelmann: German art historian who criticised the Bourbon excavations at Pompeii and Herculaneum in his open letter to M. le Comte de Brühl.

Index

Figures in **bold** refer to illustrations: figures by page number, plates by Roman numeral.